VANGUARD SERIES

EDITOR: MARTIN WINDROW

ANTI-TANK HELICOPTERS

Text by STEVEN J. ZALOGA *and* GEORGE J. BALIN

Colour plates by STEVEN J. ZALOGA

OSPREY PUBLISHING LONDON

Published in 1986 by
Osprey Publishing Ltd
Member company of the George Philip Group
12–14 Long Acre, London WC2E 9LP
© Copyright 1986 Osprey Publishing Ltd

British Library Cataloguing in Publication Data

Zaloga, Steven J.
    Anti-tank helicopters.—(Vanguard
    series; 44)
    1. Antitank missiles   2. Helicopters
    I. Title   II. Balin, George   III. Series
    358'.18   UG1312.A/

    ISBN 0-80545-697-5

Filmset in Great Britain
Printed through Bookbuilders Ltd, Hong Kong

Authors' Note

In a logical departure from the normal subject of the
Vanguard series, this title reviews the tank's newest,
and perhaps most deadly, enemy. The anti-tank
helicopter has only emerged since the early 1970s,
though its basic elements, the armed helicopter and
the anti-tank missile, have been around for several
decades. Anti-tank missiles can be fitted to nearly any
sort of helicopter; rather than present a 'lawnmower
catalogue' of types, we have focused instead on the
major dedicated anti-tank helicopters, and the actual
combat use of these machines to date.

The authors would like to thank a number of
friends for their invaluable help. Joe Bermudez
provided his usual thorough help on Syrian affairs.
Paul Boyer provided his unique collection of photos of
the NUH-1B which permitted the detailed illustration
shown here. Jim Loop provided helpful material on
Soviet helicopters, Art Loder on French helicopters,
Yoav Efrati on Israeli helicopters, and Leif Hellstrom
on Iraqi helicopters. The authors would also like to
thank the public affairs offices of the US Army,
especially Col. Charles Steiner in New York, and Bob
Lessels at Aberdeen Proving Ground for their help in
obtaining photos.

Introduction

On the morning of 2 May 1972, American and South Vietnamese troops were reeling back towards Kontum under the weight of the North Vietnamese Army's Easter offensive. Leading the NVA forces on the road outside Kontum was an M41A3 light tank captured earlier from the ARVN (Army of the Republic of Vietnam). The Chaffee crew were unaware of the appearance of a single NUH-1B helicopter just above the horizon. The gunner on board the Huey, Warrant Officer Carroll W. Lain, gathered the tank into the sights of his XM26 airborne TOW fire control system, and fired a single TOW anti-tank missile. The missile struck the tank, gutting it in an enormous fireball. This was the first recorded case of a tank being destroyed in combat by a guided missile-firing helicopter.

By 1972 neither helicopters nor guided anti-tank missiles were particularly novel. Primitive helicopters were used during the last year of the Second World War. In 1945 the Germans had developed an early guided anti-tank missile, the X-7 *Rotkappchen*, though it is unclear if it saw any combat use. The mating of these two new weapons took nearly three decades, however, as the technologies matured and as their tactical virtues came to be appreciated. Today, many military analysts consider the anti-tank helicopter to be potentially the most dangerous of all the AFV's adversaries.

Armed helicopters first began to appear in the 1950s. Some US Army helicopter crews in Korea lashed bazookas on to their machines. The French Army's 2nd Helicopter Group began experimenting with machine gun-armed helicopters during the fighting in Algeria as a means of protecting the lumbering transport helicopters. In 1956 Col. Jay Vanderpool, who headed the Combat Development Office at the US Army Aviation School at Ft. Rucker, 'borrowed' four helicopters to experiment with a variety of armament combinations in the provisional Aerial Combat Reconnaissance Platoon. In the Soviet Union, the Mil bureau began efforts to develop a machine gun package to arm the new Mi-4 troop transport. Interest in armed helicopters grew in parallel with interest in the use of helicopters for air mobile tactics.

The US Army was the most active advocate of airmobile concepts in the early 1960s, and was the first armed force to experiment with, and to field, a divisional-sized airmobile unit. The rôle of armed helicopters in this unit was that of airborne artillery. It had become evident to the Howze Board, which was organised in 1962 to study Army requirements in this field, that a heliborne division would suffer from serious fire support weaknesses if relying only on conventional artillery. A certain amount of towed artillery could be lifted by existing helicopters, but this was hardly adequate. On the other hand, helicopters could carry 2.75-in. unguided rockets in large cluster pods which could substitute for conventional artillery in many rôles. Nevertheless, the US Army did not anticipate developing a dedicated attack helicopter, preferring instead an adaptation of a normal utility machine. In 1962 Bell Helicopters proposed the D255 Iroquois Warrior, an attack helicopter based on HU-1 Iroquois components; and in 1963, Kaman offered its UH-2 Tomahawk. The US Army showed only lukewarm interest. These early airmobile division concepts did not seriously consider the anti-tank requirements of the unit. The US involvement in the war in Vietnam was growing, and undoubtedly the US Army had this rôle in mind for the new airmobile units, rather than employment in a Central European contingency.

The First Anti-Tank Helicopters

France was the pioneer of anti-tank helicopters. In the late 1950s, as a result of their experiences in Algeria, the French Army's ALOA (*Aviation Légère de l'Observation Artillerie*) devised experimental helicopter mountings for the Nord Aviation SS.10 missile. Nord Aviation was not entirely satisfied with the results, leading to the development of the improved SS.11 missile, which proved to be the first practical heliborne anti-tank missile. The US Army was very interested in the French programme, and in 1958 a US team visited Camp de Mailly to examine the SS.10 helicopter missile systems. The

US Army decided to adopt the SS.10 and SS.11 for both ground and helicopter launching. In August 1958 the US Army received its first missile-firing helicopters, a pair of Bell OH-13H machines with four SS.10 missiles each. The main problem with both the French and American helicopters was the lack of an adequate sighting system. The US Army delayed operational employment of anti-tank helicopters until the SS.11 missile became available in the early 1960s, and until an adequate sight could be fielded. The French Army followed a similar course.

The French Army was the first to field operational anti-tank helicopters. In 1963 their 1st Armoured Division received Alouette IIIs fitted with the SS.11 and a new stabilised, roof-mounted sight. The US Army began deploying the limited-standard XM-11 SS.11 launcher on HU-1As, but the first standardised system did not become available until July 1964 in the form of the improved M22 system. Like the XM-11, the M22 mounted six SS.11s (called AGM-22B in US Army service). The M22 system originally used an XM-55 sight derived from the Air Force P-61 system, but this was later superseded by the XM-58 anti-oscillation sight. This armament system was deployed to Vietnam in 1965 on board UH-1B Hueys, and was first used operationally in October 1965. Due to the absence of enemy tanks, it was used mainly to attack bunkers and other small, hard targets.

The AH-1G Cobra Gunship
The initial deployment of US airmobile units to Vietnam in the early 1960s quickly revealed their considerable combat value in an unconventional war of this type. Likewise, the armed helicopter notion proved a successful adjunct to the use of the helicopter in the troop carrying rôle. The most common armed helicopters were the 'Hogs', based on Bell UH-1 Hueys which carried a bewildering variety of gun, rocket- and grenade-launcher systems. Although very useful, many of the weapon

In Vietnam there was little call for anti-tank missiles, leading to improvised mountings like this portion of an M22 launcher attached to an XM-3 2.75-in. rocket launcher called the 'Maxwell System' after its inventor. In this fashion, both the SS.11 and the more useful 2.75-in. rocket launcher could be carried. This was fitted to a UH-1B of the 1st Cavalry Division at An Khe in January 1967. (US Army)

mountings were makeshift, and US Army officers in Vietnam began to feel that a helicopter built expressly for this rôle was required.

The Army in Washington wanted a dedicated gunship that would be capable of carrying both a rapid-fire machine gun system and rocket pods, as well as carrying sophisticated sensors which would enable it to carry out its mission at night or in poor weather. High speed was preferred to reduce its vulnerability to ground fire, and it was expected to be fairly manoeuvrable. The Army's early proposals were rejected by the Office of the Secretary of Defense (OSD), which considered them overly ambitious and not sufficiently defined. This highly sophisticated attack helicopter idea eventually emerged as the AAFSS as described below. The Army realised that the AAFSS was several years off in the future, and in view of the pressing need for attack helicopters in Vietnam, decided instead to look for an 'Interim AAFSS'.

Bell Helicopters had been working on its own private ventures which it hoped would attract Army interest. In 1963 it had developed the Bell 207 Scout, a two-seat reconnaissance helicopter with an integral chin turret. This was really too small for the gunship requirement; but in 1965 it led to a resurrected version of the Iroquois Warrior, trimmed down in size, called the Bell Model 209 or UH-1G. The Model 209 was based heavily on the

UH-1, but the nose was reconfigured with a sleeker tandem seat arrangement, a chin-mounted turret, and weapons stowage on a stub winglet. This was examined by the Army and was accepted in March 1966 as the AH-1G, better known as the Cobra. The Army decided to buy an initial order of 110 Cobras in place of UH-1Bs intended for the gunship rôle. The Cobra entered service in May 1967, and the first operational units with Cobra attack helicopters appeared in Vietnam in September 1967. Through 1971, the US Army and Marine Corps acquired 925 AH-1G Cobras and 49 AH-1J Seacobras (a Marine version with a different engine and other changes), and the Cobra saw extensive combat in Vietnam.

The AH-56 Cheyenne

The Cobra was viewed by US Army Aviation as an interim attack helicopter until a more specialised aircraft could be developed. Army interest in a larger, more capable aircraft was prompted in part by long standing disputes with the US Air Force. Since the Air Force split off from the Army in 1947, there had been intermittent squabbling between the two services over control of aircraft. The Army was supposed to limit its aircraft acquisitions to types which it directly needed to carry out its tactical mission. The Air Force was to keep control of attack aircraft used to support Army troops in the field. The Army had planned to use its OV-1 and OV-10 scout aircraft for ground support, and at one time even considered acquiring small jet trainer aircraft for this rôle. The Air Force complained that the Army was wandering too far from its own turf; and finally, after a long-simmering dispute, the Army agreed to relinquish many of its fixed-wing aircraft to the Air Force in 1966. However, this agreement still left close-support helicopters under Army control. The Army was intent on developing its own support aircraft, as it was convinced that Air Force aircraft could not always be depended upon to provide tactical air support when it was required. The Army wanted some form of air support that would be available to divisional commanders to support their units in the field. (It is interesting to note that the US Marine Corps had the same

attitude about Navy air support, and persuaded Congress to fund the AV-8 Harrier jump-jet for the same type of requirement in this period.)

Development of this new helicopter had started in 1964 as the HAX (Helicopter Armored Experimental) but it was eventually re-christened FAS, and subsequently AAFSS (Advanced Aerial Fire Support System). In 1965 Lockheed and Sikorsky developed initial designs under an Army contract, and Lockheed was selected in November 1966 to proceed with the engineering design. This emerged in 1967 as the AH-56 Cheyenne. The Cheyenne was an extremely unconventional design. It pioneered a unique compound configuration, using a novel rigid rotor, stub winglets and a rear tail and pusher propeller which gave it the exceptionally high speed of 420 km/h (260 mph). Flight and weapons controls were extremely sophisticated for a helicopter. The AFCS (Automatic Flight Control System) included a terrain-avoiding radar system to permit the helicopter to be flown safely at 'nap-of-the-earth' altitudes even at night and in poor weather. The weapons controls included night vision and a laser range finder. The

The first operational use of helicopter-fired anti-tank missiles against tanks took place in Vietnam in May 1972. This NUH-1B was one of two helicopters involved in these early encounters. These carried an experimental triple TOW missile launcher, and on the front port nose can be seen the sight/tracking system used with the TOW. (Paul Boyer)

weapons were fully stabilised, and the gunner's seat traversed with the weapons. The pilot used a helmet-mounted sight with which he could direct the fire of the turret machine guns and grenade launcher merely by turning his head (should the gunner be disabled). Although it was intended mainly as a gunship, plans were laid to incorporate the new TOW missile system into the Cheyenne at a later date. Ten prototypes were built and subjected to Army trials. The crash of one prototype, and serious technical problems with the design, led the Army to cancel its planned production in 1969, and to acquire more AH-1G Cobras instead. The Cheyenne was pushed back into development, where its future was jeopardised by continuing contract disputes between Lockheed and the US Army. As the Vietnam War began to wind down, the US Congress began to show diminishing enthusiasm for costly new weapons programmes. It questioned whether it was prudent to fund the Air Force's AX (later to emerge as the A-10 attack aircraft), the Marine Corps AV-8 Harrier jump-jet and the Army AH-56, which all appeared to envisage the same rôles. The Army saw the writing on the wall. It was not entirely happy with the Cheyenne, and many felt that the experiences with helicopters in Vietnam should be more thoroughly examined before the Army pressed ahead with a helicopter that would cost about $5.4 million (programme unit cost) each. In 1972, the trouble-plagued Cheyenne programme was cancelled by the Army.

Vietnam Anti-Tank Operations

While the Cheyenne debate was going on back in the United States, the US Army was making its first efforts to develop helicopter anti-tank tactics in Vietnam. The North Vietnamese had made very little use of tanks in South Vietnam through most of the 1960s. Small numbers of UH-1Bs were shipped to Vietnam with missile launch systems for the

The AH-56 Cheyenne represented the 1960s notion of an attack helicopter. In the early 1970s, the programme ran into serious funding and technical problems, and it was abandoned in 1973. By this time, Army interest had shifted from a high-speed gunship to a tank destroyer incorporating more advanced survivability features. (Lockheed)

French-designed SS.11 (US designation: AGM/MGM-22). The SS.11-armed Hueys were occasionally used to attack hard targets like bunkers, but shortcomings in the system and a lack of armoured targets lessened interest in the concept.

The SS.11 was a first generation MCLOS (manual command-to-line-of-sight) wire-guided missile. This guidance technique was the same as that used on the original German X-7 *Rotkappchen* of 1945, though in a more mature and developed form. The MCLOS guidance required a very skilled gunner to operate. Once the missile was launched, the gunner had to gather both the missile and the targeted tank into his sighting device. Then, using a joystick control, he guided the missile into the target. These early systems could use a radio command link between the gunner's fire controls and the missile, or a wire link—the latter, in the case of the SS.11. The wire was very fine, about the thickness of a human hair, and spooled out behind the missile. It had the advantage of being jam-proof, but it limited the speed of the missile. These early MCLOS missiles proved modestly successful in their ground-launched forms; launch from a helicopter was a trickier affair. The duration between missile launch and missile impact was usually 20 seconds or more, and it was very difficult to keep the helicopter steady during this interlude. Movement of the helicopter made the gunner's task all the more difficult, even though the system was provided with an XM55 anti-oscillation sight. Early trials pointed to the need for a more satisfactory stabilised sight.

The US Army had recognised this problem somewhat earlier, but rather than develop an expensive gyro-stabilised sight for the SS.11, decided instead to pursue development of a second-generation missile with improved guidance. This emerged in 1967 as the Hughes MGM-71 TOW (Tube-launched, Optically-tracked, Wire-guided) missile. The TOW was one of the first missiles to pioneer SACLOS (semi-automatic command to-line-of-sight) guidance. On firing a SACLOS missile, the gunner needs only to place the target in the cross-hairs of his sight and keep it there. The launcher fire controls contain a tracker which

The Westland AH.1 Scout is typical of the early adaptations of light utility helicopters for the anti-tank rôle. Besides the SS.11 missile mountings themselves, a sight has been added on the port fuselage roof for the gunner. These were first adopted by the British Army in 1970. (British Army)

follows the missile after launch by means of a bright infra-red flare at the rear of the missile. The tracker passes this on to the guidance system, which automatically sends flight corrections to the missile based on where the gunner points the sight. While developing the TOW missile, Hughes Aircraft Company also decided to develop an associated helicopter sighting system which incorporated one of their new thermal-imaging FLIR (Forward Looking Infra-red) night sights. The sighting

The AH-1J Seacobra was a development of the AH-1G Cobra characterised by a new, more powerful engine. It was acquired by the US Marine Corps, as well as by Iranian Army Aviation units, as here. These Iranian Cobras were later modified with the M65 TOW sight and other features to permit use of the TOW anti-tank missile. These helicopters have subsequently been used in the Iran-Iraq war. (Bell)

system had a daylight channel that was fully stabilised to compensate for helicopter movement during the launch-hit interlude, and the FLIR sight permitted the helicopter to attack targets in the dark by passively sensing the infra-red emissions from the engine of the tank or other sources. This package was first fitted to a UH-1B in 1966 for trials. In 1971 the fully developed system was

In the mid-1970s the AH-1G and AH-1Q Cobras were upgraded to AH-1S standards with the TOW missile, engine, fire control and other improvements. These initial conversions, called Modified AH-1S, retained the curved canopy glass of the early-model Cobras. (US Army)

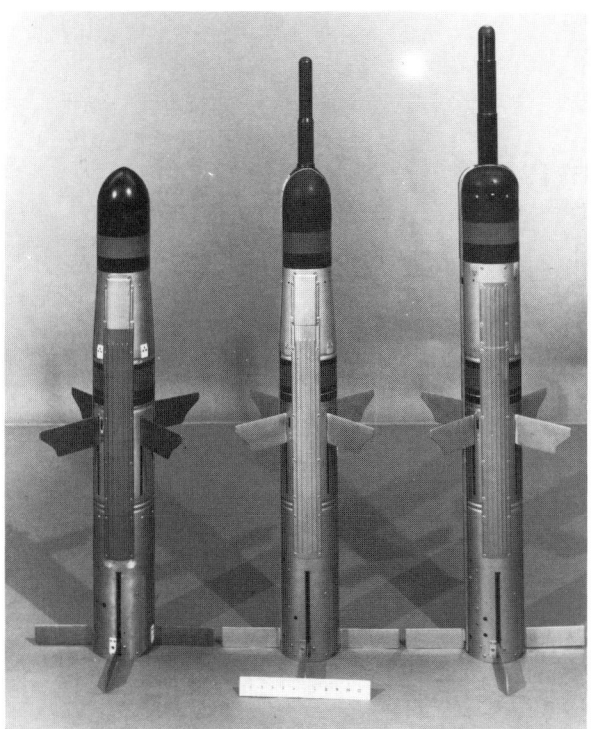

The TOW missile family tree. At the left is the basic BGM-71 TOW, used in Vietnam and many other conflicts. In the centre is the I-TOW (Improved TOW), which uses a stand-off probe in the nose to increase armour penetration. To the right is the TOW-2, which has greater range, a larger diameter warhead and the extensible stand-off probe. (Hughes Aircraft)

One of the main threats to attack helicopters flying 'nap-of-the-earth' is the presence of telephone wires and electrical powerlines. This has led to the development of wire cutters, which can be seen here being experimentally fitted to an AH-1S Cobra at Ft. Rucker, AL. This particular AH-1S is a Step 1 model, with the flat canopy glass, but still retaining the original Emerson chin turret. (US Army)

demonstrated in Germany to US and NATO forces.

When the North Vietnamese struck in April 1972, the US Army was unprepared for the large number of tanks which took part in the offensive. Fortunately, a HEAT anti-tank warhead had been developed for the 2.75-in. rocket used by the AH-1G Cobra. While difficult to use, the rocket did give the Cobra a limited measure of anti-tank capability. On 13 April 1973 AH-1G Cobras of the 3rd Brigade, 1st Cavalry Division scored the first recorded tank kill by a helicopter when they knocked out four T-54A tanks near An Loc. The Cobras managed to destroy at least 15 PT-76 and T-54A tanks and to damage a considerable number of others during the 1973 offensive. The number of rockets required to destroy a tank varied from a minimum of four to a maximum of 56.

A small number of SS.11 missiles were still in the inventory in South Vietnam, and their launchers were hastily refitted to six UH-1M helicopters. The first kill of a T-54A tank with an SS.11 took place on 21 May 1972, and a PT-76 was later destroyed. During the 1972 fighting 115 SS.11 missiles were fired, claiming only two tank kills (though several others were damaged) as well as a number of other targets.

On 12 April 1972 the TOW Programme Manager's office at the Redstone Arsenal in Alabama was requested to send the two UH-1B/XM26 TOW helicopters, which it had used in the

1971 NATO demonstration in Germany, to Vietnam on an urgent basis. The group included both military and civilian personnel and was named the 1st Airborne TOW Team or the Helicopter Anti-Tank Platoon (Provisional). It arrived on 24 April 1972, and was initially scheduled to support the ARVN troops who were besieged by NVA tanks in An Loc. In the event, the team was sent into the Central Highlands to help curb NVA attacks towards Kontum.

As mentioned earlier, the first tank kill recorded by the team occurred on 2 May 1972 on the outskirts of Kontum, when an NVA M41 light tank was destroyed. In the following two months of fighting the two helicopters fired 81 TOW missiles, knocking out 26 tanks and 33 other targets (armoured personnel carriers, trucks, barges, bunkers and bridges). The top scoring TOW gunners were CW-2 Danny Rowe with ten tank kills, and CW-3 Lester Whiteis with eight kills. When used against tanks, the helicopters averaged one kill for every two missiles fired (about 50 per

A good example of a Modernized AH-1S Step 3 during the fighting in Grenada in 1983. This model is characterised by the tubular engine exhaust IR suppressor, the 'hot brick' IR countermeasures device above the engine exhaust, the newer GE Universal gun turret, and many other improvements. (US Air Force)

cent). A later study estimated that the TOW had proven itself at least five times more effective than the earlier SS.11, but this seems to be a gross underestimation.

The Vietnam Experience Reconsidered
For the US Army, the experiences around Kontum of the 1st Airborne TOW Team marked a watershed in Army Aviation development. Not only did the operations vividly demonstrate the effectiveness of the new generation of heliborne missiles, but they came at a time when the Army was seriously questioning the rôle that armed helicopters would play in the future. With the US involvement in Vietnam winding down, the US Army began to re-examine its helicopter requirements. There was a general re-orientation away

from unconventional warfare, and a revival of interest in modernising the conventional forces stationed in Central Europe. In a European environment the gunship as a surrogate artillery system was much less relevant: there was no lack of artillery available to mechanised and armoured divisions. But the idea of a gunship as a tank destroyer struck a responsive chord. The re-orientation toward the Central European battle-field inevitably led the Army to focus once again on the gross disproportion of forces between NATO and the Warsaw Pact, especially with regards to tanks and armoured vehicles. Helicopter tank destroyers offered the hope of being able to blunt offensive tank operations at relatively low costs.

A Marine AH-1T Seacobra taking off from USS _Guam_ (LPH-9) during Operation 'Urgent Fury' off Grenada in 1983. The AH-1T is readily distinguishable from the earlier AH-1J by the presence of the M65 TOW sight in the nose, instead of the pointed nose of the AH-1J. (US Navy)

Western Developments, 1970s-80s

The early 1970s saw a flowering of interest in the use of helicopters in the anti-tank rôle. This was in part due to the proven utility of armed helicopters on the battlefield as demonstrated by the US Army in Vietnam, as well as by the arrival of the more effective second generation of anti-tank missiles like the TOW, which made the helicopter/missile combination more viable. Although there were only a handful of helicopters configured to carry the newer missiles, NATO and US units began a series of operational experiments to examine how effective anti-tank helicopters might be in a European environment. In 1972 an exercise was conducted by US and German forces near Ansbach, Germany, using AH-1G Cobras, and Leopard 1 tanks

The latest derivative of the AH-1 Cobra family is the AH-1W Supercobra developed for the US Marine Corps, which will carry the Hellfire missile. (USMC)

simulating an 'aggressor' force. The tests concluded that anti-tank helicopters were extremely successful in blunting an armoured attack, averaging 28 tank kills per helicopter lost. The tests also stressed the use of hunter-killer tactics, with light scout helicopters like the Kiowa seeking out targets for the Cobra to attack. The tests suggested that anti-tank helicopters should each carry at least eight missiles, as it was found that the number of recorded kills per missile dropped 28 per cent when only four missiles were carried: the helicopters had to continually return to rear areas to reload. Some of the observers questioned the realism of the exercise, since the helicopters were not encumbered with real missiles, and the German tankers made no particular effort to mimic Soviet tactics; nor were any ground-based air defence assets present. As a result, in 1973–74, the US Army staged more controlled tests using AH-1G Cobras and simulated Soviet tank formations. These tests suggested that expected exchange ratios between tanks and helicopters would vary from 3:1 in favour of the helicopters up to more than 14:1, depending on the size of the attacking helicopter force. The trials suggested that a formation of five helicopters was dramatically more effective than a single machine, which could only expect an exchange ratio of 3:1.

European Programmes

A British exercise conducted around the same time, called 'Hell Tank', contradicted the US findings, and found that the size of the attacking helicopter force did not dramatically change the exchange ratio between helicopters and tanks. This trial used the Scout AH Mk 1 helicopter, which had been adapted in 1970 to carry four SS.11 missiles. Nevertheless, it did conclude that anti-tank helicopters could play a significant rôle in blunting tank attacks, even with the older generation missiles.

The TOW was not the only second-generation missile to appear during this period. The Franco-German consortium Euromissile, made up of MBB and Aérospatiale, began developing a similar missile, the HOT (*Haute subsonique Optiquement teleguide tire d'un Tube*) in 1964 as a replacement for the SS.11. The German Army considered the AH-1G, Westland WG.13 and the MBB BO-105 as possible contenders for their PAH-1 (*Panzer Abwehr Hubschrauber*-1), finally settling on the BO-105P, which could carry six missiles. The French Army

This gaudily-painted Bell Helicopter YAH-63 was one of two competitors in the AAH programme. It lost out to the Hughes YAH-64. (US Army)

decided to acquire the SA.342M Gazelle for the ALAT (*Aviation Légére de l'Armée du Terre*). The French and German approaches to anti-tank helicopters showed a distinct tactical difference from the contemporary American approach, which was to go for a specialised attack helicopter with light armour protection against small arms fire. Such a helicopter also carried a gun armament to suppress enemy infantry or soft targets, and could thus be used both for close-range, direct attack with guns and unguided rockets, or long-range, stand-off attack with anti-tank missiles. The French and German armies preferred the less versatile but more economical approach of a completely unarmoured helicopter, with no additional armament, which would be used exclusively in the long-range, stand-off rôle. This tactic attempted to minimise damage to the helicopter from small arms fire by keeping the machine well away from enemy lines. These helicopters did not begin entering service until the late 1970s and early 1980s due to the prolonged gestation of the HOT, which did not enter full-scale production until 1977.

The US Approach
The US Army reached exactly the opposite conclusion as a result of the early 1970s experiments, as well as the Vietnam experience. The Americans were unimpressed with European adaptations of light scout helicopters as anti-tank

This photo shows the original conception of the Hughes YAH-64 prototype, which eventually evolved into the AH-64 Apache. (US Army)

missile carriers, feeling that the machines were too small to carry a worthwhile load of missiles, and that the missiles that were carried seriously degraded the performance of the helicopter. Furthermore, the US Army felt that under modern battlefield conditions a helicopter had to have at least some protection against small arms to survive. During the period from September 1967 through to June 1969, 563 AH-1G Cobras were hit by ground fire during the fighting in South-East Asia; however, only 57 were lost. The US Army studies did not suggest that these experiences would be typical of encounters with contemporary Soviet ground forces in Europe: indeed, they made it quite clear that much higher loss rates could be expected due to the presence of heavier weapons such as the

The AH-64 is a design of inspired ugliness. The device in the nose is the TADS/PNVS sensor used to fly the helicopter and target its weapons day or night. Under the winglets are eight Hellfire missiles. Between the two forward landing gear is the helicopter's 30mm cannon. (US Army)

ZSU-23-4 *Shilka* air defence gun vehicle. The US Army clearly preferred a more versatile attack helicopter than that offered by simply strapping anti-tank missiles to a scout machine. Apart from the need for armour the studies also concluded that attack helicopter survivability could be enhanced by incorporating special features into such designs from the outset of development. Manoeuvrability was stressed as a way to inhibit accurate hostile ground fire. Aural, radar and infra-red signatures should be reduced to make it more difficult for hostile troops to detect approaching helicopters by

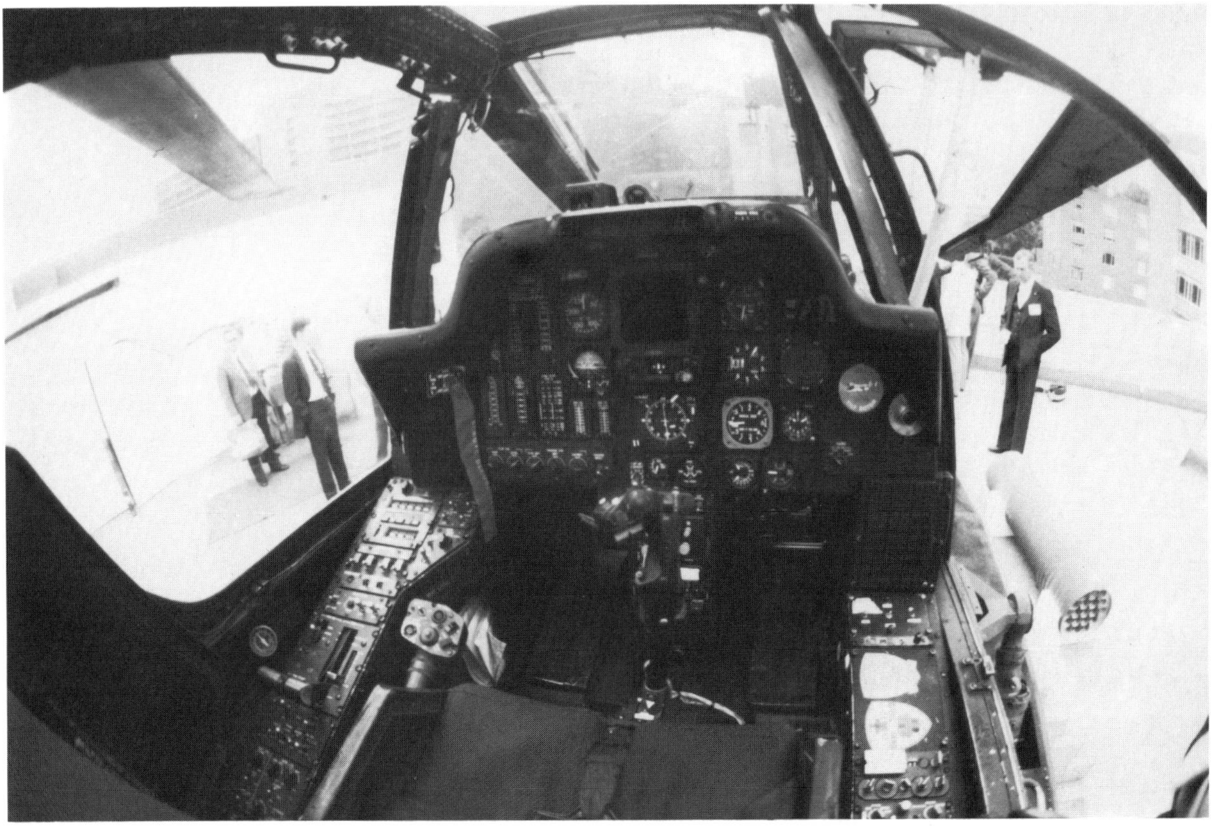

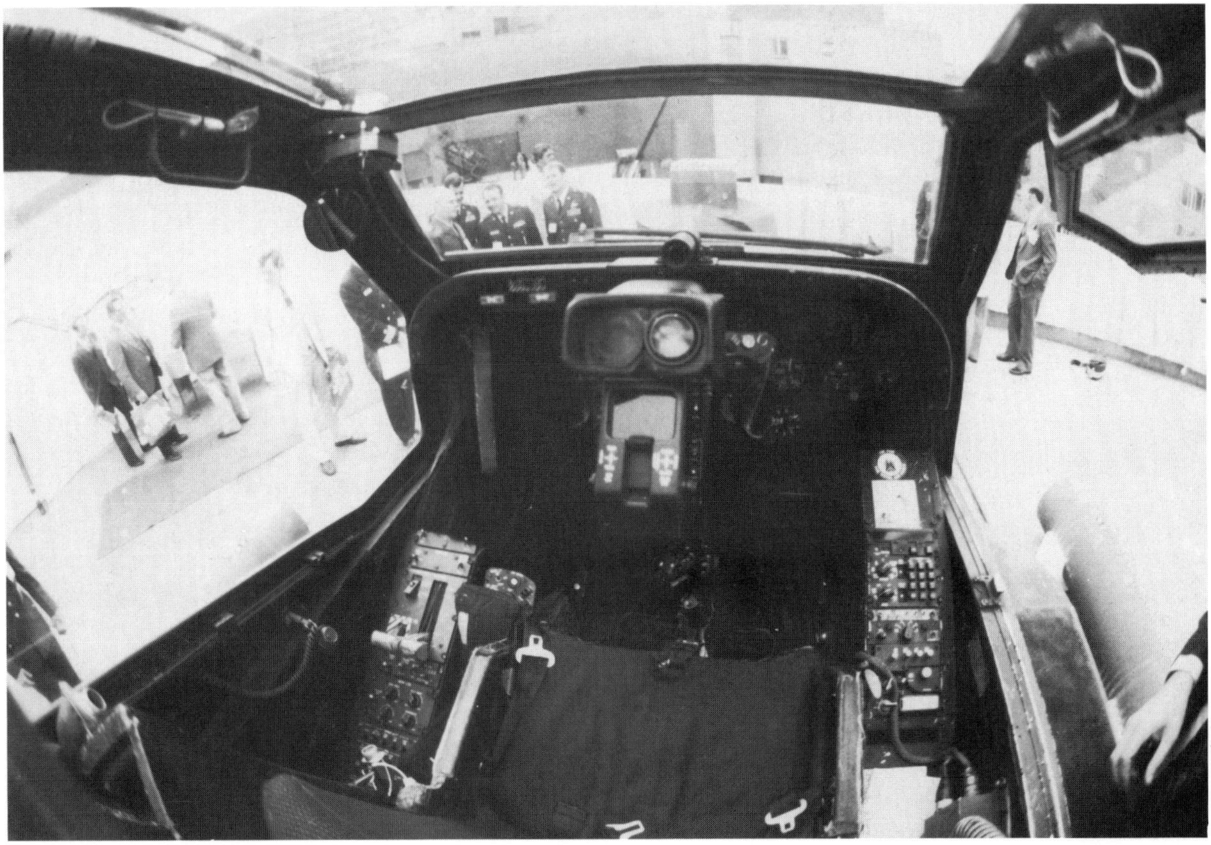

sound, or through the use of radar or other electronic sensors. A helicopter designed to operate at 'nap-of-the-earth' (NOE) reduced its vulnerability, since it was nearly impossible to detect by radar. The studies also stressed the incorporation of electronic countermeasure systems to baffle enemy air defence radars and infra-red countermeasures to protect against the new generation of man-portable infra-red-guided anti-aircraft missiles like the Soviet 9M32 *Strela* 2 (SA-7 'Grail'). Light utility helicopters like those adopted in Europe could not carry as extensive a countermeasures suite as a dedicated attack helicopter.

The US Army decided to implement these notions in two ways. First, the existing AH-1G would be modernised and adapted to carry the TOW missile. Second, a new attack helicopter would be developed to provide a more capable anti-tank helicopter in the next decade.

The AH-1G Modernisation

Modernisation of the AH-1G Cobra took place in a number of phases. The AH-1Q improvement incorporated an uprated engine, and the ICAP (Improved Cobra Armament Package) with TOW launchers and a helmet-mounted sight. The AH-1Q programme included both modification of 93 AH-1G Cobras and production of new AH-1Q helicopters, taking place from 1973 through 1977. The basic problem was that the new TOW launchers taxed the powerplant even with the improvements, degrading the helicopter's manoeuvrability. Furthermore, the fire control

Left
A view from the pilot's seat of the AH-64A Apache. The pilot sits behind and above the weapons operator: he can aim the helicopter's weapons using a helmet-mounted sight system. (Zaloga)

A view of the weapons operator's station in the AH-64A Apache. At the centre is the main weapons fire control sight and console. The helicopter can be flown from this station as well. (Zaloga)

Below
The crew of this AH-64 Apache are seen wearing the futuristic Honeywell IHADSS (Integrated Helmet and Display Sight Subsystem). This allows the Apache crew to aim and fire the helicopter weapons merely by turning their head towards the target. The helmet is electro-optically linked internally to the fire control system, which slaves the helicopter weapons to the pilot's head motion. (Bob Lessels)

system was limited to clear weather only, and in some respects was inferior to that used on the original UH-1Bs at Kontum. The AH-1Q was viewed as an interim solution until these problems could be addressed. A more extensive modernisation package was completed. The modernised helicopters were to have further engine improvements, but the most dramatic changes came in the aircraft electronics. The nose was reconfigured with the new M65 TOW fire control system, which included a fully-stabilised daylight sight. At first, AH-1Gs with the new features were to be designated AH-1R, and modernised AH-1Qs were to become AH-1S; but eventually, all upgraded helicopters came to be known as AH-1S. The first AH-1S Cobras, called Modified AH-1S, were modified from 372 AH-1G and AH-1Q Cobras in 1975–1984, and retained the standard Cobra canopy. The new production AH-1S Cobras, called Step 1, used a flat-plate canopy in order to reduce reflections, which could give away their positions at long ranges while hovering. The production of the new AH-1S began in 1976, and modifications were gradually introduced into these

new production Cobras as well. The improved AH-1S Step 2, also called Up-Gun AH-1S, has the new GE Universal Turret, a wings stores management system and other improvements, and totals 98 aircraft. The Step 3, also called Modernized AH-1S, includes fire control improvements, an air data system, a Doppler navigation system, IFF transponder, a new infra-red jammer, an infra-red suppressor over the engine exhaust, secure-voice communications, and other improvements. Production of this batch of 99 helicopters was completed for the US Army in 1981, but an additional 55 were ordered for the US Army National Guard in 1983.

Marine Cobras

After ordering a small batch of AH-1Gs for attack helicopter familiarisation in Vietnam, the US Marine Corps ordered a total of 69 AH-1J Seacobras, which were powered by twin Pratt & Whitney PT6T-3 engines. These were not configured for the TOW missile, although AH-1J Seacobras ordered later by Iran did have fittings for the TOW. The Marines began ordering the improved AH-1T Seacobra in 1974, totalling 57 aircraft to date. The AH-1T Seacobra is a Marine counterpart to the AH-1S, having a variety of engine and weapon improvements, including the M65 TOW sight and provisions for the TOW missile. The Marines did not become involved in

A production AH-64A Apache on initial trials along the Colorado River in 1984. The elaborate engine exhaust system is configured to cool the hot gas as much as possible to reduce its vulnerability to heat-seeking missiles. The Apache incorporates other infra-red countermeasures which go a long way towards eliminating the threat of IR-guided missiles such as the Soviet SA-7 'Grail'. (McDonnell Douglas)

One of the first of the US Army's anticipated 675 AH-64A Apache attack helicopters. This particular machine is armed with Hellfire missiles and the newer Hydra 70 2.75-in. rocket launchers. (McDonnell Douglas)

the US Army Apache programme (see below), and, as a result, developed a further upgrade package for the Cobra in the early 1980s to take advantage of new defensive electronic developments, powerplant upgrades, and the new Hellfire anti-tank missile. These features are incorporated into the new AH-1W (formerly AH-1T+) which was first ordered in 1985.

The AH-64 Apache

Development of a successor to the ill-fated Cheyenne began in September 1972, shortly after the earlier programme had been cancelled. The new programme was termed AAH (Advanced Attack Helicopter). In 1973 the Army selected two firms to build competitive prototypes of the AAH: Bell Helicopters, offering the YAH-63, and Hughes Helicopters, offering the YAH-64. The conception behind the AAH differed considerably from the Cheyenne. The Cheyenne was intended as an

The Mi-24 'Hind-A' was originally powered by the Isotov TV2-117 engine, and had the tail rotor on the starboard side of the tail. This view shows one of these early 'Hind-As', armed with two UB-32 rocket pods and launch racks for the *Falanga* guided anti-tank missile. (US Navy)

airborne artillery fire support aircraft which would attack targets at high speed, overhead, from an altitude of several hundred feet with rockets and gunfire. The AAH was envisioned primarily as an anti-tank helicopter, attacking its targets from several kilometres away in a very low altitude hover. Much less stress was placed on high speed, and instead the emphasis was shifted to the

development of a stable launch platform with improved survivability features. This included much more strenuous requirements for protection against small arms fire; reduction of IR, aural and radar signatures; and the incorporation of electronics and infra-red countermeasures systems. Central to the design of the new AAH was the Hellfire missile.

The Hellfire was a third-generation missile, using semi-active laser guidance. It was based on the earlier but ill-fated Hornet programme. The helicopter's fire control system included a laser designator which projected a narrow beam of laser light against the targeted tank. Some of this light reflects off the tank, and the Hellfire's sensitive seeker picks up this light, and homes in on it. The target can be laser-illuminated either by the helicopter launching the missile, or by a ground

The most common series production model of the Mi-24 *Gorbach* is called 'Hind-D' by NATO. This 'Hind-D' of the Czechoslovak Air Force clearly shows the nose barbette with a 12.7mm 'Gatling'-type machine gun, a radio antenna for *Falanga* missile guidance, and the armour-covered port for the infra-red night viewing system. This helicopter is not fitted with the infra-red suppression gear seen on Mi-24s in Afghanistan. (Eastfoto)

designator, or by another helicopter. The main advantage that this sytem offers over a wire-guided missile like the TOW is that, without the burden of the trailing wire, the missile can be designed to travel at much higher speeds and for a greater distance. The Hellfire is supersonic, having a maximum speed of about 385 metres per second and a maximum range probably in excess of five kilometres. (The TOW has a maximum speed in the high subsonic range of about 280 m/sec, and a maximum range of 3.7km.) From launch to target impact at a range of 2.5km, the TOW would take 12 seconds, while the Hellfire would take seven seconds. A 'fire-and-forget' version of the Hellfire, the IIR Hellfire, was under development in the late 1970s and early 1980s. This used a cooled infra-red seeker that was sensitive enough to pick up a tank even without its engine running. After locking the seeker on to its target, the helicopter could fire it and fly away, not having to loiter and guide the missile to target, as must be done with the TOW and laser-guided Hellfire. This programme was cancelled due to costs and technical problems; but this type of helicopter-launched missile is likely to appear in the next decade, using imaging infra-red (IIR) or millimetre wave radar (mm wave) guidance.

In December 1976 the Hughes YAH-64 was selected as the winner of the AAH competition. The new helicopter was designated the AH-64 Apache, in keeping with the US Army tradition of naming helicopters after American Indian tribes. The AH-64 was nearly cancelled in 1978 during budget battles in the US Congress, and again in 1981 its future was in question. The US Department of Defense considered whether the European approach might not be better after all, and instead of developing an attack helicopter, a simpler stand-off anti-tank helicopter might suffice: it was proposed that an anti-tank version of the UH-60 Blackhawk transport would be well suited to this rôle. However, the US Army vehemently resisted this suggestion, and contended that the Blackhawk alternative was deficient in terms of speed, mission endurance, vulnerability to ground fire and other factors, and that it would not save the Army significant costs through time. In spite of its high price tag ($11.9 million unit cost in 1984), the Army succeeded in winning approval of the programme, and the first production aircraft were funded by the US Congress in 1982 and delivered in 1985. Training on the Apache began in 1985, and the first unit was planned to become operational at Ft. Hood, Texas, in 1986.

The Soviet Experience

Although helicopter development in the Soviet Union has kept pace with that in Europe and the USA, Soviet military use of helicopters has been conservative. According to a Soviet engineer who worked for the Mil Design Bureau, the development of the first major Soviet military transport helicopter, the Mi-4, was initiated in response to US use of helicopters in Korea[1]. Likewise, Soviet Army interest in attack helicopters was spurred on by US use of attack helicopters in Vietnam. Helicopters in the Soviet Army are under the control of the Air Force, not the Ground Forces; and, not surprisingly, the Air Force showed little interest in developing helicopters for a rôle already fulfilled by strike aircraft[2].

In the early 1960s there was some experimentation with very primitive gunship tactics. The Mi-4A helicopter developed at this time had a single Afanasyev TKB-481 machine gun mounted in a gondola below the fuselage. It had a very limited

The pilot station of an Mi-24 'Hind-D'. The pilot is protected by 6mm of armour, and the front panel of the cockpit is bullet-resistant glass. (Eastfoto)

[1] Lev Chaiko, *Helicopter Construction in the USSR*, (Delphic Associates: Leesburg, VA, 1985)

[2] The Soviets do not use the term 'Army' in the European sense. The Soviet Army consists of the Ground Forces (comparable to the British or US Army), the Air Forces, the Strategic Missile Force, the National Air Defence Force and the semi-autonomous Air Assault Force

Another view inside the cockpit of an Mi-24 'Hind-D', looking from the rear troop compartment forward towards the pilot's station.

The programme appears to have been given a significant boost by the border fighting between Soviet KGB Border Guards and the Chinese Army along the Ussuri River in the eastern USSR in 1969—the worst in a series of clashes which had been going on for several years. It was of special concern to the Soviet Army, since the vital Trans-Siberian Magistral Railway line was not far from the Chinese frontier at this point. The Trans-Siberian was the only major communication link between the central USSR and the Far Eastern military districts, and carried most of the major military supplies: Chinese border actions could effectively cut off the Pacific bases in a single lunge for the railway. As a long-term solution to the problem the Soviets began adding the Baikal-Amur Magistral (BAM) railway spur, which took over 15 years to complete. In the short term, military forces in the region were bolstered.

field of fire, and was of dubious utility. The Mi-4A could also be fitted to carry bombs. In parallel with programmes in France and the USA, there were also experiments to fit rockets, guided anti-tank missiles and gun pods to helicopters, including both the small Mi-1 utility helicopter and the Mi-4 transport. These projects do not seem to have borne much fruit, and Soviet helicopter doctrine remained oriented mainly towards the transport rôle.

In the late 1960s Soviet interest in attack helicopters was stirred by the US AAFFS programme. The Mil bureau seems to have been especially enamoured of the Sikorsky entry, which eventually resulted in the S-67 Blackhawk prototype, and appears to have proposed developing a Soviet counterpart. This initially met with little interest. Mikhail Mil himself showed some personal interest in this concept, and used the American programme as a lure to entice the Soviet Army to fund a similar effort. The Helicopter Directorate of the Soviet Army's General Staff issued a Technical-Tactical Requirement (TTT) for the development of an attack helicopter to the Mil bureau in the summer of 1968. The programme had an air of urgency about it, and the Mil bureau decided to use modified elements of the new Mi-8 helicopter, including the rotor system, with an upgraded reduction gearbox and more powerful engines. Two types of tail rotor configurations were tested, a conventional system and a fenestron system (like that used on the Gazelle).

A closeup of the nose of an East German 'Hind-D' showing the rather massive fire control system in the gunner's station used for aiming the *Falanga* anti-tank missile and machine gun barbette. The helmet flash is white on red.

The KGB, which is responsible for protecting the Soviet frontier, became extremely interested in the notion of an armed helicopter that could be used to patrol along the distant Soviet-Chinese frontier and repulse Chinese incursions. The KGB requirement that the helicopter carry a small squad of troops may have been one of the factors in the Mil bureau's decision to add a troop compartment to the new attack helicopter design. This feature was also present on the Sikorsky S-67 Blackhawk, but is otherwise unique in attack helicopter designs.

The first prototypes of the Mi-24 flew in 1970, and were probably built in a small batch at the Panki experimental facility. The original version was intended mainly as a fast artillery rocket platform. Its small stub wings could carry the usual S-5 57mm rocket in UB-32 pods. Surprisingly, it was armed only with a single Afanasyev 12.7mm machine gun, flexibly mounted in the front canopy. Armour was rudimentary: the floor and seats were protected by 6mm of steel armour, but the canopy was unarmoured glass. As a result, side protection was offered in the form of a sliding panel of steel armour, which blocked off the crew's side view when in use! This version of the Mi-24 was called the 'Hind-B' by NATO. Very small numbers of

A training *zveno* of four Mi-24s at the Syzran Air Force Academy. It will be noted that this is a training version of the 'Hind-D', lacking the machine gun barbette in the nose. These helicopters still have the launch racks for the older *Falanga* missile. (Sovfoto)

these entered Soviet Air Force (VVS) service in the early 1970s, probably only for operational trials. They were followed in 1972 by the first series production version of the Mi-24, called the 'Hind-A' by NATO. The 'Hind-A' had a reconfigured stub winglet with wider chord; this was apparently added to give the helicopter more lift and a higher cruise speed. The 'Hind-A' was also the first version to include a winglet end-plate for mounting the *Falanga* guided anti-tank missile (US/NATO designation AT-2 'Swatter'). Although the 'Hind-A' was originally powered by the Isotov TV2-117, these were soon replaced by the more powerful TV3-117R, and the tail rotor was shifted from a right-side pusher to a left-side tractor style.

Actual operational experience with the 'Hind-A' improved Soviet Air Force understanding of the tactical requirements of attack helicopters. In many respects, the 'Hind-A' had serious tactical short-comings. The machine gun position offered very little traverse, and was nearly useless. The armour configuration was hopelessly inadequate, and

23

machine gun rounds could readily penetrate the sides. The rotor was vulnerable to small arms fire, and the weak tail boom led to accidents. The main rotor and power train, though nominally having a life of 2,000 hours, had an effective life closer to a tenth of that figure.

A major redesign of the Mi-24 began around 1972, with the aim of curing these deficiencies. By this time the Mil bureau had received components of American AH-1s from Vietnam, possibly even an entire helicopter. It is not clear what effect this had on the design effort. This redesign programme was probably managed by Mil's successor, Marat Tishchenko. The nose was redesigned in a tandem configuration like that on the AH-1 Cobra or AH-56 Cheyenne. Armoured glass was added to the forward canopies, and the crew were enclosed in an armoured 'bathtub', protected against small arms fire. The new version was designed to be proof against 7.62mm ammunition, with some ability to survive heavier fire. The front armament system was completely redesigned, adding a 12.7mm multi-barrel machine gun in a small traversing

A flight of Mi-24 *Gorbachi* at the Syzran Air Force Academy undergoing periodic maintenance. The considerable size of the *Gorbach* is very evident in this view. (Sovfoto)

barbette, flanked on either side by the *Falanga* radio command antenna and a new night sensor port. This version, dubbed 'Hind-D' by NATO, also had considerable improvements in infra-red suppression and powertrain subsystem ballistic protection. The 'Hind-D' was first seen by the West in 1976, although it was probably in service earlier. It soon earned the nickname *Gorbach* ('Hunchback') in VVS service, due to its distinctive profile.

Concurrent with the development of the *Gorbach* was a new helicopter-launched anti-tank missile. The *Falanga* (AT-2 'Swatter') was a first generation MCLOS guidance type using a radio command link. For use on the Mi-24 it was upgraded with a SACLOS guidance system, resulting in the AT-2c 'Swatter-C'. The 'Swatter-C' was an interim solution until a new missile could be fielded. It was a relatively old weapon which had first entered service in 1960. It had a range of 3.5km, but was fairly slow, taking 23 seconds to reach its maximum range. This long launch-hit interlude is particularly important on Soviet attack helicopters, since, unlike US and most NATO attack helicopters, anti-tank missiles are launched during forward motion, not from hover.

Indeed, due to the large stub winglet, which is

1: Bell UH-1B, 2/20th Artillery, US 1st Air Cavalry Division; An Khe, Republic of Vietnam, July 1967

2: Bell NUH-1B, 1st TOW Team; Republic of Vietnam, May 1972

A

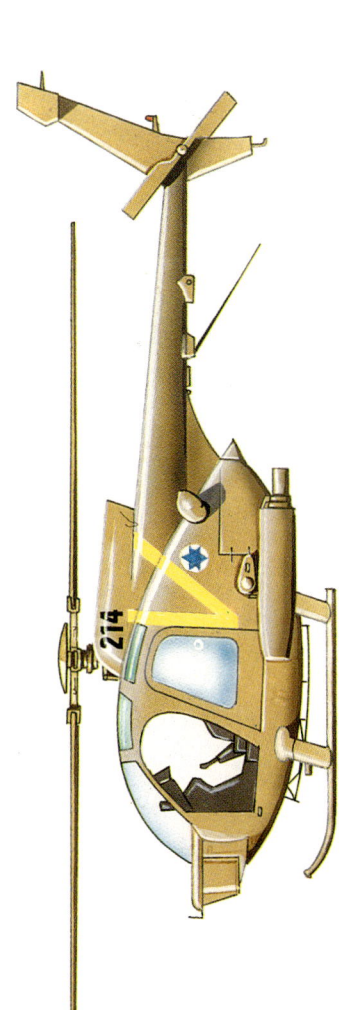

1

2

1: Hughes 500 MD Defender, Israeli Heyl Ha'Avir; Lebanon, 1982
2: Bell AH-1S Cobra, Israeli Heyl Ha'Avir; Lebanon, 1982

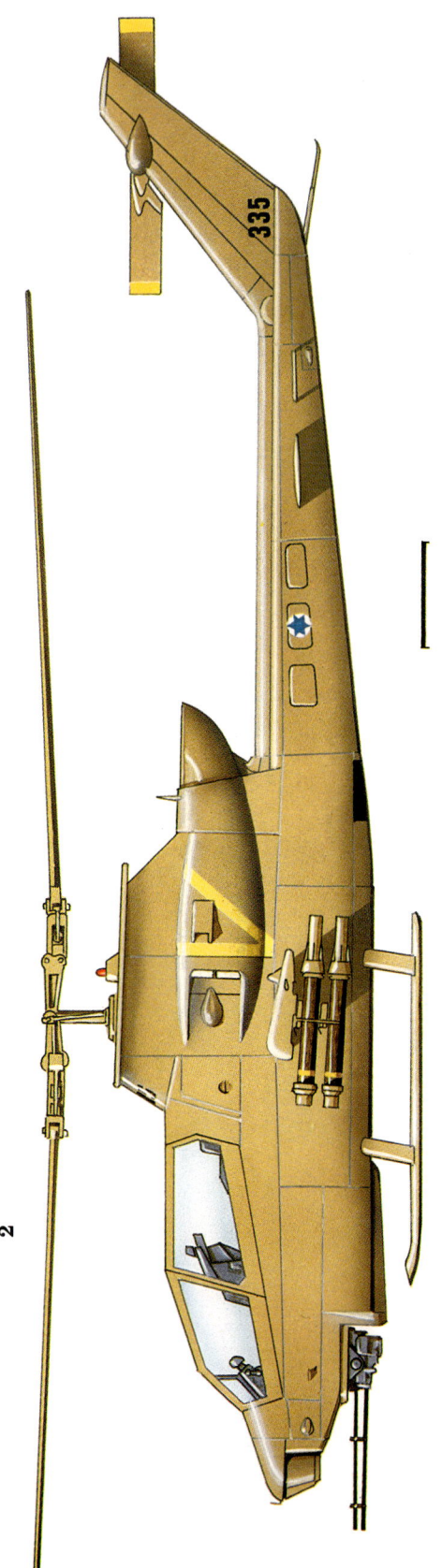

B

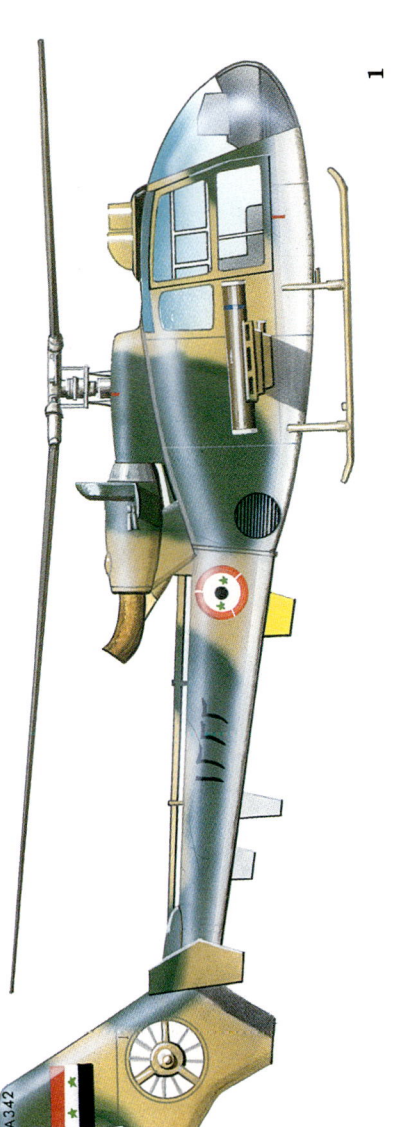

1: Aérospatiale SA.342M Gazelle, Syrian Attack Helicopter Regt.; Lebanon, 1982

2: Bell AH-1J Cobra, Iranian Army Aviation; Iran, 1979

C

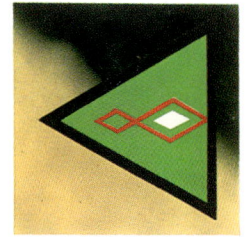

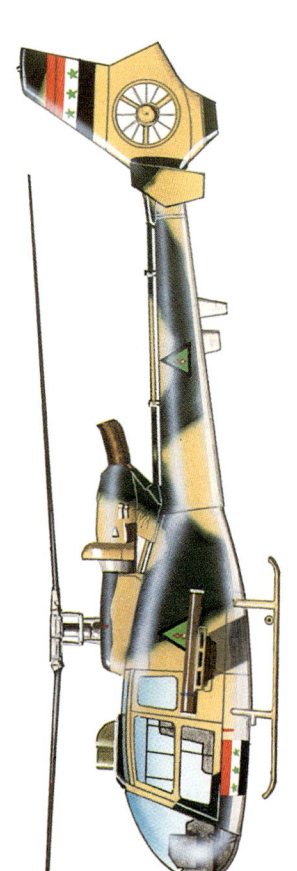

1: Aérospatiale SA.342M Gazelle, Iraqui Air Force, 1984

2: Mil Mi-24 'Hind-D', Iraqui Air Force, 1984

1

2

D

1: WSL–Swidnik Mi-2M, Polish Air Force, 1980
2: Mil Mi-24 'Hind-E', Soviet FA-VVS; Druzhba Exercise, 1982

1

2

E

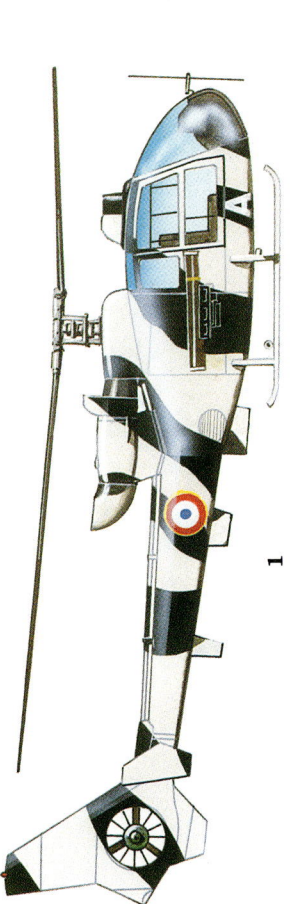

1

2

1: Aérospatiale SA.342M Gazelle, 2ᵉRHC, French Army ALAT; Operation 'Manta', Chad, 1983

2: Mil Mi-24 'Hind-A', Libyan Arab Air Force, 1982

F

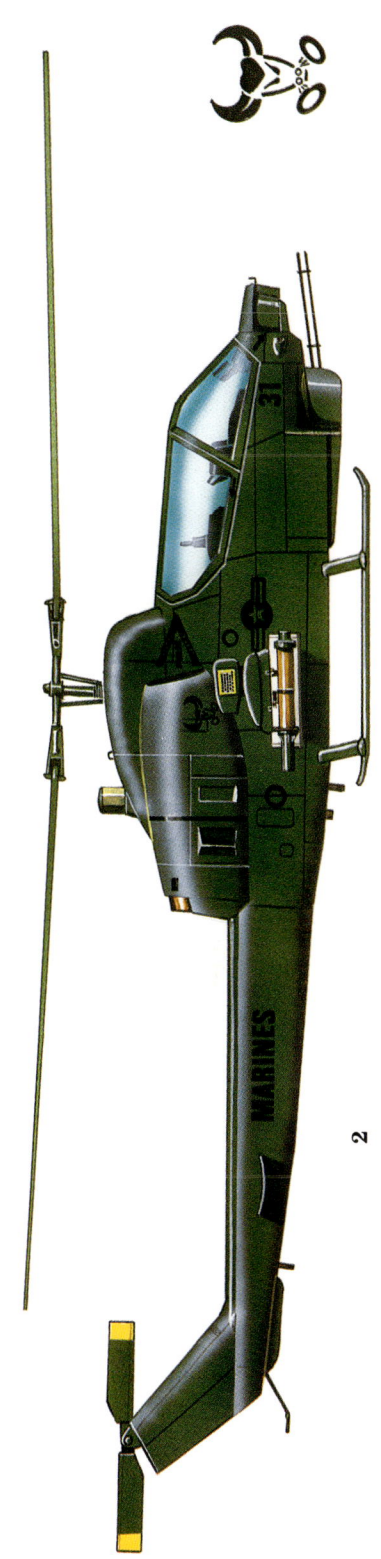

1: Mil Mi-24 'Hind-D', Sandinista Air Force; Nicaragua, 1985
2: Bell AH-1T, US Marine Corps HML-261; Operation 'Urgent Fury', Grenada, 1983

1

2

G

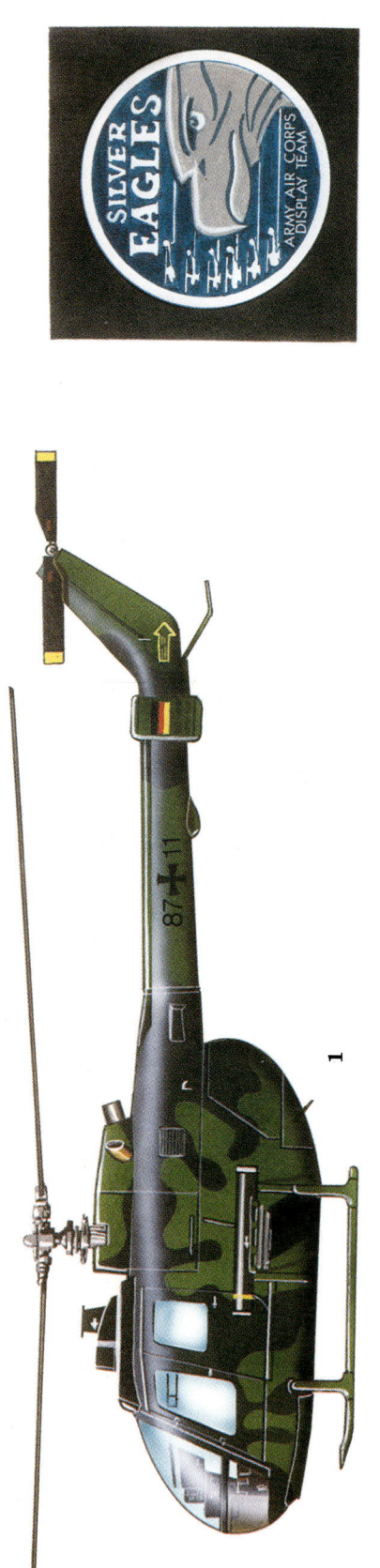

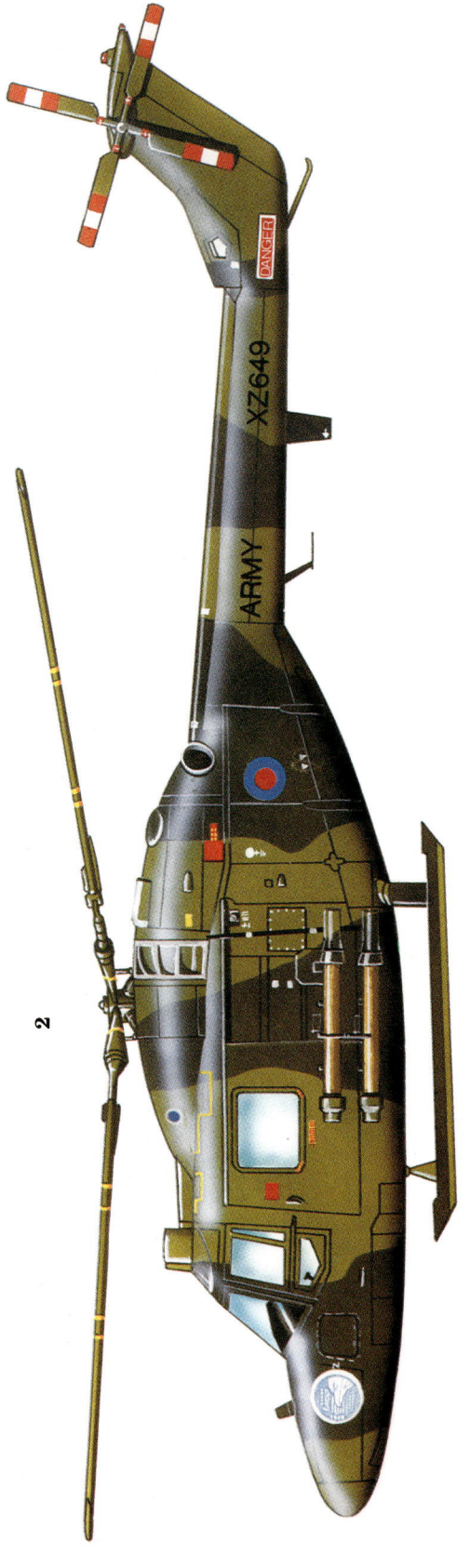

1: MBB PAH-1, Bundesheer Panzer Abwehr Regt. 36; FRG, 1984
2: Westland Lynx AH.1, Lynx Conversion Flight 'Silver Eagles', British Army Air Corps, 1982

The only unclassified photo released, purportedly showing a 'Hind-E' with the AT-6 'Spiral' anti-tank missile. This seems extremely unlikely, as the missile tube pictured seems hardly large enough for a missile with the performance attributed to the 'Spiral'. (US Army)

right in the middle of the rotor downwash, the Mi-24 has virtually no ability to hover out of ground effect. This is a conscious off-shoot of the Mi-24 design, which stresses high-speed performance (like the AH-56 Cheyenne). The new missile, known by the US/NATO codename AT-6 'Spiral', entered service around 1974 for operational trials. The 'Spiral' is a second generation SACLOS guidance missile using a radio command link. Its main advantage over the *Falanga* is higher speed, greater accuracy and an improved warhead. The 'Spiral' has a maximum range of 5km, and can reach this range in 11 seconds. The Mi-24 was modified to carry the guidance equipment for this missile, and this version is designated as 'Hind-E'. It was first spotted in Germany in 1978, but probably had been in Soviet service since 1976.

The initial version of the 'Hind-E' was armed with the same 12.7mm machine gun barbette as the 'Hind-D'. At the Druzhba-82 exercise in 1982 an improved type, with the barbette removed and twin 23mm autocannons added to the starboard fuselage side, was first seen. The rationale for this new armament configuration is not clear. It has been suggested that the new weapons presage the use of the Mi-24 in helicopter-vs-helicopter fighting. It may also have been adopted to give the Mi-24 some ability to knock out light armoured vehicles, including lightly armoured air defence gun vehicles like the German *Gepard*.

Although the Mi-24 has been the centre of attention in Soviet anti-tank helicopter development, other projects were undertaken. In the 1970s, some Mi-8 'Hip' helicopters were configured to permit use of the 9M14M *Malyutka* (AT-3c 'Sagger-C') SACLOS guidance anti-tank missile: this version is called 'Hip-F' by NATO. Production of the Soviet Mi-2 is undertaken by WSK-Swidnik in Poland, where some experimentation in anti-tank derivatives was undertaken in the early 1970s. The Mi-2 attack helicopter featured four 9M14M *Malyutka* missiles on pylon launchers, a flexibly mounted PKM 7.62mm machine gun added to the side cargo door, and a fixed, forward-firing PKM added to the lower port fuselage. These armed Mi-2Ms were adopted by the Polish Air Force, and may be in use elsewhere in the Warsaw Pact. It is interesting to note that some export models of the Mi-24 are also fitted for the smaller and shorter-ranged 'Sagger' instead of the 'Swatter', and this may account for the Mi-25 designation used for certain export Mi-24s.

Anti-Tank Helicopters in Combat

The first known combat use of **Soviet** anti-tank helicopters came in 1979 in Afghanistan. In August of that year a number of rebel Afghani soldiers commandeered some tanks and attempted to attack the presidential palace in Kabul. A flight of Mi-24 *Gorbachi* were sent to stop the tanks, and destroyed them using anti-tank missiles and S-5 rockets. The Mi-24 has subsequently been used with considerable success in Afghanistan against the *mujahideen*, but is seldom used in an anti-tank rôle in the fighting there.

Israel acquired American attack helicopters in the 1970s, including AH-1Q, AH-1S, and, later, the Hughes 500MD Defender. The Israeli helicopters are controlled by the *Heyl Ha'Avir* (Air Force), and are grouped in anti-tank helicopter squadrons. Israeli helicopter doctrine stresses the use of anti-tank helicopters in the defensive rôle. The primary impetus for Israel acquiring these helicopters had been the realisation, after the 1973 Golan Heights fighting, that anti-tank helicopters could serve as a very potent, highly mobile anti-tank reserve to stop

An Mi-24 'Hind-E' of the later type with the twin 23mm autocannon on the starboard fuselage side and launch mountings for the AT-6 'Spiral' anti-tank missile. This helicopter was taking part in the 1985 Kavkaz-85 exercise. Note that this version lacks the nose gun barbette, like the training version of the 'Hind-D'.

armour that had broken through ground defences. In spite of this doctrinal approach, the Israeli armed forces decided to deploy their attack helicopters in the 1982 fighting in Lebanon, where the tactics inevitably were of a more offensive nature.

Details of the 1982 air war are still sketchy, and there is a good deal of conflicting information about the number of losses suffered by both sides. According to Israeli sources, the AH-1S Cobras and the Defenders knocked out 28 tanks (including some T-72Ms), 16 armoured personnel carriers and 13 other vehicles, in addition to a number of bunkers and other targets. The TOW missiles were credited with a better than 70 per cent probability of hit and kill during these operations. Some accounts have indicated that the helicopters accounted for 60 per cent of the Syrian armoured vehicles knocked out in the Bekaa valley fighting.

Israeli helicopter losses have not been officially disclosed, but are believed to have totalled four attack helicopters: two to Syrian ground fire and two to friendly fire. One of the friendly fire casualties is believed to have been a Defender which was mistaken for a Syrian Gazelle and was hit by tank fire.

Israeli *Heyl Ha'Avir* officers have expressed mixed feelings about the use of attack helicopters over Lebanon. Many officers felt that conventional ground attack aircraft were more effective than helicopters, since they could be used to attack targets deep inside Syrian-held territory. The low-flying attack helicopters were vulnerable to small arms fire, especially the Defenders, and could only be used along the periphery of the battleline, attacking from stand-off distances. However, many officers admitted that this is how Israeli doctrine had planned to use them anyway, and in Lebanon they were often used over 'unswept' territory, which was against normal tactical doctrine. Israeli tankers had a very different attitude to attack helicopters after having been subjected to Syrian attacks. Tanks have a very hard time spotting helicopters;

and even the helicopter's Achille's heel—its easily identifiable sound—is of little help to tank crews due to the din of armoured vehicles in motion. Helicopters can appear from nowhere and hit several tanks before their presence is even recognised.

The **Syrian** Air Force first acquired attack helicopters in 1977 in the form of 18 Aérospatiale SA.342L Gazelles. These were first fitted with the AS.12 missile, an improved version of the SS.11, as an interim measure pending production of the far superior HOT missile. Early in 1978 the Syrians ordered two more squadrons of Gazelles, totalling 36 aircraft. In 1981 these were supplemented by 12 Mi-24 'Hind-D' attack helicopters from the USSR. They were first used in February 1982 to help suppress the Hamah uprising in Syria. The attack helicopters were first used in combat in the fighting for Mt. Lebanon on 25–27 April 1982. (The Syrian Air Force lost two 'Hinds' to Israeli aircraft prior to the 1982 war in Lebanon.) Before the outbreak of that war the attack helicopters were organised into an attack helicopter regiment, with one squadron of 'Hinds' and four squadrons of Gazelles. It would appear that most of the unit was based at Al-Mazzah airbase, with a single Gazelle squadron at Al-Ladhiqiyah.

Although the 'Hinds' probably saw some action in the 1982 Lebanon War, it was the Gazelles which made the greatest impression on the Israeli tankers due to their superior HOT missiles. Syrian tactics called for co-ordination between the helicopters and Syrian Army units. The aim was to ambush or tie down Israeli armoured formations with tank fire or close range commando attack, at which point the Gazelles would be called in. The Gazelles operated in flights of four, usually in two pairs. The helicopters would pop up to fire, and usually attempted to use Lebanon's hilly terrain to find their way to the flanks or rear of the Israeli columns. Because the Gazelle has a roof-mounted sight, the helicopters could often use terrain obstruction to hide while guiding their missile to target. Actual Israeli casualties from the Gazelles have not officially been made public, but some sources indicate that only two tanks and one M-113 were destroyed by HOT fire. Syrian Gazelle losses were heavier than Israeli losses, with at least seven helicopters shot down by ground fire (both friendly and hostile) and by aircraft. At least one of the

A Hughes 500 MD Defender of the Israeli Air Force. This anti-tank version of the Hughes 500 carries four TOW missiles, and is fitted with the missile tracker/fire control in the sensor pod on the port side of the nose. (Hughes Helicopter/McDonnell Douglas)

An Israeli AH-1S armed with four TOW missiles. This view underlines the small target that an anti-tank helicopter presents during 'pop-up' attack. (Government Press Agency)

Gazelles was shot down by tank fire from a Merkava of the Israeli 7th Armoured Brigade—though there is some dispute as to whether this was intentional, or simply the result of the Gazelle happening to be in the wrong place at the wrong time. There are also reports that one of the Gazelles was shot down by an AH-1S Cobra using a TOW anti-tank missile. The Israelis found two of the Gazelles nearly intact, and managed to salvage a single machine from the wrecks by cannibalising parts.

Probably the most extensive use of anti-tank helicopters has taken place in the Gulf War between Iran and Iraq which has been dragging on since 1980. The **Iraqi** Air Force is equipped both with Mi-24 'Hind-Ds' and French SA.342M Gazelles. The **Iranian** Islamic Republic Air Force is equipped mainly with AH-1J Seacobras acquired during the Shah's reign. Very few details of the use of these helicopters have been reported. Reputedly, an Iraqi 'Hind' shot down an Iranian F-4 Phantom fighter which strayed too near. The Iraqis have also claimed that they have brought down several Cobras using Milan anti-tank missiles. The Iraqi Gazelles and 'Hinds' are used for fire support as well as anti-tank operations; the Gazelles are sometimes fitted with HOT missiles on one side and Matra unguided rocket clusters on the other to cover either eventuality.

Anti-tank helicopters have also figured in various coup attempts and civil wars. In the early 1970s the

Spanish Army used Alouette III helicopters with SS.11 missiles in the fighting against guerillas in Spanish Morocco. During an attempted coup by the Republican Guard in **Cameroon** in 1984, using Cadillac Gage V-150 armoured cars, loyalist forces used the country's two SA.342M Gazelle helicopters fitted with HOT missiles to attack and destroy six of these vehicles. Mi-24 helicopters apparently played a part in the short civil war in **Yemen** in January 1986.

Anti-tank helicopters have figured in a number of other wars in the 1980s. The US Marine Corps used four AH-1T Cobras of HML-167 with TOWs in **Grenada**, though these were not used against armoured vehicles, but against such targets as machine gun nests. The US Army also had AH-1S Cobras in Grenada, but these too saw no anti-armour use. During operation 'Manta' in 1983 the French Army sent small detachments of the 2ᵉ and 5ᵉ RHC (*Régiment d'Helicoptères de Combat*) to **Chad** to provide flank and anti-armour protection to other elements of the French force. The SA.342M Gazelles proved very effective in this rôle, being able to range over considerable distances in the desert to keep an eye out for Libyan armoured columns. Although the Gazelles never engaged Libyan armour, one Gazelle encountered a Toyota light truck mounting a light automatic cannon in the rear bed, and blew it in half with a single HOT missile. The **Libyan** Air Force operated Mi-24s in Chad, and at least one was shot down by French forces. These two examples show the value of anti-tank helicopters to expeditionary forces, which seldom have enough transportation available to bring in significant quantities of tanks to deal with whatever hostile armour might be encountered. Instead, the more easily transportable anti-tank helicopters can provide a highly flexible defence against tanks, as well as proving useful in general fire support and scouting missions.

Contemporary Anti-Tank Helicopter Tactics

The tactical concepts for the use of anti-tank helicopters vary widely from army to army, due in part to their relative novelty, and also to the variety of helicopters used in these roles. The use of unarmoured, lightweight helicopters like the Gazelle, PAH-1 or Defender mandate certain tactics, while the use of larger and more versatile attack helicopters such as the Mi-24, AH-1S or AH-64 make other approaches more feasible. The better to illustrate the considerable diversity of approaches in the use of attack helicopters, five armed forces will be discussed here briefly.

US Army Anti-Tank Helicopter Doctrine
The US Army has long been in the forefront of attack helicopter development, and deploys the largest and best-equipped force in NATO. Under the ARCSA III organisation of 1977, each mechanised and armoured division was equipped with a combat aviation battalion and an armoured cavalry squadron, totalling 172 helicopters of which 51 were AH-1S anti-tank helicopters. The Cobras were deployed in two attack helicopter companies in the combat aviation battalion (42 Cobras) and a further nine were attached to the air cavalry troop of the armoured cavalry squadron. The AH-1S Cobras are normally teamed with the OH-56A Kiowa scout helicopter: American doctrine stresses the need for scout-attack helicopter co-ordination. This stems in part from the Vietnam experience. The US Army does not feel that it is tactically justifiable to use the more expensive and capable attack helicopters for scouting, since scout helicopters traditionally suffer the highest casualty rate of helicopters in any military rôle. Rather, the scout helicopters, as well as neighbouring ground forces, locate and identify likely targets; the attack

helicopters can then consider the optimum route of attack.

Attacks from the flank and rear are preferred, but the TOW missile can destroy most contemporary tanks even when used against the thick front armour. Attack tactics stress the use of 'nap-of-the-earth' (NOE) approaches to minimise exposure to air defences like ZSU-23-4 Shilkas. The attack is usually executed from the hover, even though the stabilised M65 sight on the AH-1S permits attacks while evasive manoeuvres are undertaken. US attack helicopter doctrine is more aggressive than that of most other NATO armies. This is made possible by the use of more robust machines which

An Iraqi SA.342M during the 1984 fighting with Iran. This helicopter is fitted to carry the HOT missile, which is not loaded in this view.

also carry a much more elaborate defensive electronics suite. US attack helicopters have less to fear from man-portable anti-helicopter missiles like the 9M32 *Strela* 2 (SA-7 'Grail') than most other NATO anti-tank helicopters due to the provision of exhaust cooling systems, 'hot brick' infra-red jamming systems, flare countermeasures and missile warning systems. US attack helicopters also carry a more comprehensive ECM suite, including radar warning devices to alert the crew to the presence of radar-directed guns like the ZSU-23-4.

In the early 1980s the US Army began reorganising its heavy divisions under the 'Division 86' plan. This plan has not yet been completed in all details, particularly with regard to attack helicopter deployments. The initial plan called for the deployment of a combat aviation brigade with each armoured or mechanised division. This brigade would include two attack helicopter battalions, each with 21 AH-1S or AH-64 Apache attack helicopters, 13 OH-58D AHIP scouts and three UH-60 Blackhawk utility helicopters. The battalions each have a headquarters company and three attack helicopter companies, each attack company having seven attack helicopters and four scouts. There are a further eight attack helicopters in the divisional armoured cavalry squadron.

The US Army is currently debating whether it might not be better to concentrate more attack helicopters in larger corps-level units. These would be used as operational reserves to smash armoured breakthroughs, or to engage in massed anti-armour attacks. Under this revised plan, the divisional combat aviation brigade would be trimmed back to only a single attack helicopter battalion. The current configuration of the corps-level aviation brigades includes three attack helicopter battalions. These brigades each have 231 helicopters, including 63 attack helicopters and 54 scouts.

British Anti-Tank Helicopter Doctrine
The British Army is one of the few in NATO to deploy anti-tank helicopters in its division; however, these divisional helicopter units are tiny

A Hughes 500 MD Defender of the Kenyan 50th Air Cavalry. Light anti-tank helicopters like this are popular in many smaller armies, as they cost a fraction of the price of the dedicated anti-tank helicopters such as the AH-64 Apache or Mi-24. (Hughes Helicopter)

compared to the US example. The British Army was slow in adopting anti-tank helicopters, and prefers the economy approach of adapting a light utility machine to this rôle. The Westland Scout fitted with SS.11 missiles is still in service, augmented by the newer Westland Lynx AH.1 with the TOW missile. An armoured division has an organic army aviation regiment, with two helicopter squadrons. One squadron, used for reconnaissance, is equipped with 12 Gazelles; the other anti-tank squadron is equipped with Lynx AH.1 with TOW (or in some cases, with the earlier Scout). As in most other NATO armies, there are also army aviation regiments at corps level. The Lynx would be used in a defensive fashion, using 'pop-up' attack tactics at stand-off range to minimise casualties from ground fire. The Lynx would perform its own scouting, as there are minimal provisions to use the hunter-killer tactics favoured by the US Army.

The British Army has suffered from very poor funding of its army aviation branch, and is among the most thinly equipped of the major NATO armies in this respect. It is embarrassing to note that even the Italian Army is pursuing its own dedicated anti-tank helicopter, the Agusta A.129 Mongoose, while there are no comparable British programmes beyond evolutionary developments of the Lynx, e.g. Lynx 3. Some consideration has been given to license-producing the Mongoose at Westland.

French Attack Helicopter Doctrine
The French Army's aviation branch, ALAT, has been one of the pioneers of anti-tank helicopters. However, over the years it has not enjoyed the level of funding received by US Army Aviation, and has generally fallen behind both in the scale of deployment and in the development of new equipment. ALAT had planned to replace the older Alouette III (armed with the dated SS.11) with the newer SA.342M Gazelle. However, recent plans to expand the number of attack helicopter regiments will probably mean that the Alouette will remain in service until the next-generation HAC-3G helicopter arrives. The French Army no longer deploys anti-tank helicopters at divisional level, preferring to concentrate them in corps-level combat helicopter regiments, the regiment consisting of six squadrons with ten helicopters each. A modernised

A new trend in light anti-tank helicopters is the provision of a mast-mounted sight, as on this Hughes 530MG Defender. This type of sight enables the unarmoured helicopter to seek out and attack targets while hiding behind trees and terrain obstructions with only the sight projecting above the horizon. This Defender has just fired a TOW missile. (McDonnell Douglas)

regiment with new equipment would have one transport squadron with Puma helicopters; a support squadron with SA.341F Gazelles; a protection (gunship) squadron with SA.341F Gazelles mounting twin 20mm guns; and three anti-tank squadrons, either with Alouettes or with the newer SA.342M Gazelle with six HOT launchers. Besides the regiments attached to each corps, three combat helicopter regiments belong to the 4th Airmobile Division. The 4th Airmobile Division is one of the formations allotted to the new strategic intervention force, the FAR (*Force d'Action Rapide*) which could be employed overseas (as in Chad) or in a Central European contingency.

French tactical doctrine is fairly aggressive considering the modest capabilities of the Gazelle. The French Army presumes that in the event of a NATO engagement in Central Europe, it might have to make a fighting advance into Germany. The attack helicopter squadrons would be expected to act in the vanguard of the force, and not be limited to defensive, stand-off tactics as practiced in most other NATO armies. In view of these tactical preferences, it is not surprising that France has been an active participant in the Franco-German Aérospatiale/MBB third generation attack helicopter programme. The French Army plans to adopt two versions of this new helicopter: the HAP gunship (*Helicoptère d'Appui et de Protection*: Support and Defence Helicopter) to replace the SA.341F,

and the HAC-3G anti-tank helicopter (*Helicoptère Anti-Char-3ᵉ Generation*: Third Generation Anti-Tank Helicopter) to replace the SA.342M Gazelle. These new helicopters, and their German counterpart the PAH-2, will be the equivalent of the AH-64 Apache in many respects. The anti-tank versions will be armed with the PARS-3/Trigat missile, a replacement for the current HOT.

German Anti-Tank Helicopter Doctrine

The German *Bundeswehr* was slower even than the British Army in adopting anti-tank helicopters. The BO-105P was selected for the PAH-1 requirement (*Panzer Abwehr Hubschrauber-1*: Anti-tank Helicopter-1), and entered service in the early 1980s. The first fully operational PAH-1 unit, the *HFlgRgt 16* (Army Aviation Regiment 16) was deployed in 1984 as part of *HFlgKdo 1* (Army Aviation Command 1) at Celle-Wietzenbruch. *Bundeswehr* tactical doctrine represents the other tactical extreme from that of the US Army: the *Bundeswehr* units use very light helicopters, with no armour, very little defensive electronics and no night-fighting capability. The tactics are purely defensive, and no scout helicopters are used to assist in targeting. The German doctrine stresses peacetime training to familiarise the crews with local terrain. The *Bundeswehr* feels that in time of war the helicopter regiments would be very familiar with the local terrain, and would be able effectively to exploit terrain features to approach hostile tank units. All attacks would be conducted from stand-off ranges where small arms fire would be ineffective, and even *Shilka* fire would be out of range.

As is the case almost everywhere else in Europe, the *Bundeswehr* deploys very few attack helicopters at divisional level (in contrast to US practice), and concentrates most of these assets at corps level. The sole exception to this is the *HFB 6*, a helicopter squadron with 21 PAH-1s attached to the *6.Panzergrenadier Division*. The corps level regiment, now designated *PzAbwRgt* (*Panzer Abwehr Regiment*:

The new Lynx 3 displays many of the features being adopted by the most recent generation of anti-tank helicopters. It is fitted with a mast-mounted sight to assist in target tracking while masked behind terrain features. Above the canopy is a wire cutter to prevent entanglement in powerlines. Beside the main anti-tank missiles are a pair of podded anti-helicopter missiles to deal with opposing attack helicopters. (Westland Helicopters)

Anti-Tank Regiment) has a total of 60 helicopters consisting of 56 PAH-1 and four unarmed BO-105 utility machines. The attack helicopters are divided into eight flights, each with seven helicopters. The *Bundeswehr* has 170 PAH-1 and 42 more on order from MBB.

The *Bundeswehr* plans to modernise its anti-tank force in the 1990s with the PAH-2, the German equivalent of the French HAC-3G which is being jointly developed between Aérospatiale in France and MBB in Germany. The PAH-2 is a lightly armoured, dedicated attack helicopter along American lines. Its appearance will mark a decided improvement in *Bundeswehr* anti-tank helicopter capabilities, and may signal a shift to a more aggressive anti-tank doctrine.

Soviet Anti-Tank Helicopter Doctrine

The Soviet Army attaches most of its attack helicopters to the Frontal Aviation branch of the Air Forces (FA-VVS) in an organisation sense, though they are usually under the control of the Ground Forces in an operational setting. The basic attack helicopter formation is the Attack Helicopter Regiment, equipped with 40 Mi-24s and 20 Mi-8T

One of the most popular light anti-tank helicopters is the Aérospatiale SA.342M Gazelle, configured for HOT missiles. This particular Gazelle belongs to a Combat Helicopter Regiment of the French Army's ALAT. (Aérospatiale)

armed transports. These regiments are deployed at army level (equivalent to NATO corps). The regiment is divided into three squadrons, with the two attack squadrons each having 20 Mi-24s. Until recently, the attack squadrons had flights (*zveno*) of four helicopters each, acting in pairs; however, in recent years the flights have been reduced in size to three helicopters each.

Soviet attack helicopter tactics differ dramatically from those of NATO due to the technical differences between Soviet and NATO designs. Nearly all NATO armies stress the use by attack helicopters of stand-off, 'pop-up' tactics, with the helicopters launching their missiles from a low-altitude hover. Because the Mi-24 cannot easily be hovered out of ground effect, Soviet tactics stress the use of anti-tank missiles while the helicopter continues in forward flight. In this respect, Soviet tactics are somewhat more akin to traditional fixed-wing aircraft ground attack tactics. However, like NATO, Soviet tactics stress 'nap-of-the-earth' flying, and the Mi-24 is equipped with a radar altimeter to assist in accurate low-altitude flying.

The shift in *zveno* organisation from four to three machines was prompted in part by shifting tactical considerations in Soviet helicopter doctrine. The Soviet Air Force feels that in a Central European confrontation one of the main enemies of anti-tank helicopters would be other anti-tank helicopters. Modern anti-tank helicopters are very difficult to shoot down using most existing ground-based air

defences, the dedicated attack helicopters like the Mi-24, AH-1S and AH-64 Apache being fitted with infra-red suppression equipment which makes them much less vulnerable to infra-red guided anti-aircraft missiles. Radar-guided anti-aircraft missiles are nearly useless at very low altitudes due both to 'ground clutter', which interferes with their guidance, and to their dependence on proximity fuses which cannot be used effectively too near to the ground. Most gun systems, like the ZSU-23-4, have ranges shorter than the stand-off range of the missiles carried by attack helicopters.

The new *zveno* organisation presumes that two helicopters would be used to execute the ground attack mission while the third would maintain a slightly higher altitude and act as cover for the attacking pair. This helicopter would probably be configured like the newer Mi-24 'Hind-E', with the twin 23mm autocannons. These guns could be used against enemy attack helicopters, or to attack other anti-helicopter weapons including man-portable air defence missile teams, air defence missile or gun batteries, and other targets. The Soviets are likely to have already tested air-to-air anti-helicopter missiles, perhaps derived from the new SA-14 'Gremlin' man-portable, laser-guided, air defence missile.

This model shows the most recent configuration of the proposed MBB PAH-2 for the German *Bundeswehr*. MBB's partner in this co-operative Franco-German venture, Aérospatiale, has designed a French anti-tank version, currently known as the HAC-3G. (MBB Helicopter)

These tactics are being studied with interest by NATO, and parallel developments on this side of the Iron Curtain. The US Army is developing an air-to-air version of the Stinger missile for helicopter fighting; France is developing a version of the Mistral, and Sweden is developing a version of the RBS-70.

Soviet experience with attack helicopters in Afghanistan is likely to broaden Soviet appreciation for this class of weapon. It would seem likely that divisional attack helicopter units will eventually be strengthened. Throughout the 1970s, the Ground Forces' Army Aviation service was limited to divisional helicopter detachments with Mi-2s and

The German *Bundeswehr* uses a version of the BO-105P armed with HOT missiles for its PAH-1. This overhead view shows the related BO-105CB, which is configured with eight TOW launchers and other changes from the PAH-1. (MBB Helicopter Corporation)

Mi-8s for utility duties. In the 1980s, some of the tank and motor rifle divisions began to receive a more potent helicopter squadron with 18 machines divided into six flights, each with three helicopters. The composition seems evenly divided between Mi-24 attack helicopters, Mi-2 utility/scout helicopters, and Mi-8T transport/support helicopters.

The Mi-24 has not been regarded as a complete success by the Soviet Air Force. Its aerodynamic performance was constrained by basing it on the Mi-8T transport. Furthermore, experience with the Mi-24 has provided the Soviet FA-VVS with a clearer appreciation of the technical features it desires in an attack helicopter. In 1978 the design bureau under Marat Tishchenko at the Moscow Helicopter Factory (M.L.Mil) began work on a successor, the Mi-28. Prototype testing began in 1980, initial series production in 1983, and operational trials (in Afghanistan and the USSR) in 1985. The Mi-28 was designed from the outset as an anti-tank helicopter, with considerable stress on weapons fire control modernisation, and improved aircraft survivability features. To date, very little information has appeared on this new helicopter except for the drawing which was released by the US Department of Defense in 1985 (and reproduced in this book). The Mil bureau has also worked on a smaller two-to-four-man utility helicopter to replace the Mi-2. One of its intended rôles would be as a light-weight anti-tank helicopter. However, as far as is known, the Soviet Air Force has not agreed to series production of this design.

Increasing attention is being paid to the use of attack helicopters to fight hostile attack helicopters. This shows a test fitting of the Swedish Bofors RBS-70 anti-aircraft missile, mounted on a modified Westland Lynx helicopter. (Bofors)

The Plates

(Because of the widely different dimensions of the helicopters illustrated on these plates, no true common scale can be adopted; but the two machines on each single plate are to common scale in each case.)

A1: Bell UH-1B, 2/20th Artillery, US 1st Air Cavalry Division; An Khe, Republic of Vietnam, July 1967
This Huey is finished in the more colourful style of Army markings common in the early days of the Vietnam War, before such markings were toned down. The basic scheme is overall olive drab with chrome yellow markings, and a black anti-glare panel. Some helicopters of this unit carried a battalion insignia on the nose. The SS.11 missile is also olive drab with yellow markings (indicating a live high explosive warhead), and the launch assembly is light grey.

A2: Bell NUH-1B, 1st TOW Team; Republic of Vietnam, May 1972
This NUH-1B (serial number 62-12553) is the highest-scoring anti-tank helicopter to date, having knocked out 18 of the 26 tanks destroyed by this provisional unit in 1972. The scheme is unique to this unit, and appears to consist of forest green and black on the upper surfaces and grey on the undersurfaces. The other helicopter in this unit (64-12254) used a different scheme which seems to have had additional field drab patches. The unit insignia was carried on the nose, and is shown here in the inset drawing to the left. On the front of the TOW launchers was a small, stylised white skull and cross-bones, which is shown in detail in the inset drawing to the extreme right. This helicopter also carried a red and white decal of the popular Crumb cartoon slogan 'Keep On Truckin''. The kill markings are red for tanks, and forest green outlines for trucks and barges: these are shown in the three inset drawings on the right. The barge and truck markings are almost invisible; they are in two vertical rows under the tank markings, four barges

and eight trucks. The other helicopter used yellow kill markings.

B1: Hughes 500MD Defender, Israeli Heyl Ha'Avir; Lebanon, 1982
This Defender is finished in the pale sand-grey common to all Israeli helicopters. The yellow 'V' insignia was applied as a form of national identification for Operation 'Peace for Galilee'. The Israeli national insignia is shown in the inset drawing.

B2: Bell AH-1S Cobra, Israeli Heyl Ha'Avir; Lebanon, 1982
This Cobra is finished in much the same fashion as the Defender. The Israeli Air Force uses small cartoon unit insignias on the tail of the AH-1S, but

these are classified and censored from most photos: hence, regretfully, the blank here. The individual aircraft number is repeated in black at the front of the engine fairing.

C1: Aérospatiale SA.342M Gazelle, Syrian Attack Helicopter Regiment; Lebanon, 1982
This Syrian Gazelle is finished in what appears to be a standard Aérospatiale desert delivery scheme of yellow sand and medium green, with pale grey undersurfaces. To this has been added the Syrian national insignia, and the helicopter number in black. This is the helicopter recovered by Israeli forces after the fighting.

C2: Bell AH-1J Cobra, Iranian Army Aviation; Iran, 1979
The Iranian Cobras were delivered in this scheme of earth yellow and field drab with grey under-surfaces. The crest on the nose is that of the Army Aviation, and has 'Army Aviation' in Arabic at the base of the insignia. Since the overthrow of the Shah the Imperial Iranian Army Aviation acronym has

One of the major advantages of a large and powerful helicopter like the AH-64 Apache is that its configuration can be readily modified to take advantage of changing tactical conceptions. Here, an AH-64A has been modified to carry two AIM-9L Sidewinder missiles besides its usual weaponry. This configuration was developed in an effort to interest the US Marine Corps in the Apache. (McDonnell Douglas)

been replaced by IRIAA (Islamic Republic of Iran Army Aviation); but some photos would seem to indicate that the old 'IIAA' is still retained on some Cobras. This Cobra is shown with the new M65 TOW sight refitted. The Army Aviation crest is shown in detail, inset, above right.

D1: Aérospatiale SA.342M Gazelle, Iraqi Air Force, 1984
This Iraqi Gazelle is finished in much the same fashion as the Syrian machine illustrated as Plate C1, in a standard desert delivery scheme, but with dark green substituting for medium green. The application of the Iraqi national insignia seems to vary somewhat from helicopter to helicopter: it is shown inset, right.

D2: Mil Mi-24 'Hind-D', Iraqi Air Force, 1984
This Iraqi Mi-24 is finished in one of the standard Soviet delivery schemes of earth yellow and field drab with pale blue-grey undersides: to this has been added the Iraqi national insignia. Note that

The latest Soviet attack helicopter is the Mi-28, known to NATO as the 'Havoc'. This artist's conception, released by the US Department of Defense in 1985, is one of the few sources of information on this new helicopter. It is interesting to note that its general configuration is not significantly different from that of the current generation of NATO attack helicopters such as the AH-64 Apache, A.129 Mongoose, PAH-2 or HAC-3G. (US DoD)

on some export delivery helicopters, the tail warning sign has been painted on in English.

E1: WSL-Swidnik Mi-2M, Polish Air Force, 1980
The Polish Air Force uses this colourful three-tone camouflage scheme on some of its helicopters. The markings are fairly simple, including the national insignia and helicopter tactical number.

E2: Mil Mi-24 'Hind-E', Soviet FA-VVS; Druzhba Exercise, 1982
This Mil-24 is finished in one of the standard delivery schemes for Mil-24s, earth yellow and dark green. Soviet tactical numbers on helicopters vary in colour, but the significance of this is not known,

The US Army currently plans to develop a new light helicopter to replace the current OH-58 AHIP. Unlike the AHIP, it will be manned by a single crewman, and will be configured for anti-tank operations, as shown in this sketch of the Boeing Sikorsky entry in the LHX programme. The LHX will be optimised for helicopter fighting as well as scouting.

though it is suspected to be a squadron colour system. Some Soviet 'Hinds' and other tactical aircraft carry the red insignia shown to the right of Plate E1: this may be a Frontal Aviation insignia showing unit proficiency.

F1: Aérospatiale SA.342M Gazelle, 2e RHC, French Army ALAT; Operation 'Manta', Chad, 1983
The ALAT Gazelles arrived in Chad in their normal metropolitan scheme of *vert armée*. This was not altogether suitable for desert operations, leading to improvised camouflage schemes like this one, most of them applied by using mud, not paint. The camouflage obscures the normal white squadron tactical markings, leaving only the first letter of the three letter code, 'A', showing. To the right of the helicopter is the insignia of the *Force d'Action Rapide*.

F2: Mil Mi-24 'Hind-A', Libyan Arab Air Force, 1982
This Libyan Mi-24 is shown in the normal delivery scheme for the 'Hind-A', grey and dark green. Some of the Libyan 'Hinds' seem to use a different scheme, with the upper surface camouflage extending underneath. It carries the simple green disc insignia of the Libyan Air Force.

G1: Mil Mi-24 'Hind-D', Sandinista Air Force; Nicaragua, 1985
This Sandinista Mi-24 is painted in a variation of the usual Mi-24 delivery scheme, the green colour being paler than is normally the case. The tail warning marking is in Russian, and the helicopter carries the normal Sandinista national insignia and fin flash. Note that this helicopter is fitted with a 'hot-brick' system to protect it against the SA-7 missiles used by the *Contra* rebels.

The sting of an anti-tank helicopter comes from its missile, with its massive shaped-charge warhead. The effect of this warhead against a tank is amply demonstrated by this photo of an impact on a derelict M47 at the White Sands Proving Ground in the US. (US Army)

G2: Bell AH-1T, USMC HML-261; Operation 'Urgent Fury', Grenada, 1983

US Marine Bell AH-1Ts in 1983 were finished in this very drab scheme of overall forest green with black markings. The unit insignia, a raging bull, was painted on the side of the engine cowl, and is shown in detail on the inset drawing. Other markings include the rescue arrows near the cockpit, black circles around refuelling points, the national and service insignia, and the warning chevron in front of the engine intake. The device above the stub wing is a countermeasures dispenser, and this helicopter ('31') is armed with twin TOW launchers and 2.75-in. rocket launchers, the latter painted white.

H1: MBB PAH-1, Bundesheer Panzer Abwehr Regiment 36; Federal Republic of Germany, 1984

PAH-1s and BO-105s of the *Bundesheer Flieger*

The Agusta A.129 Mongoose is the first dedicated European attack/anti-tank helicopter. Its features bridge the gap between the older and less capable AH-1 Cobra and the larger and more elaborate AH-64 Apache. (Agusta)

Kommando were finished in this standard pattern of medium green and black. The national insignia and other markings are in subdued black except for warning markings.

H2: Westland Lynx AH.1, Lynx Conversion Flight 'Silver Eagles', British Army Air Corps, 1982

The Lynx is finished in the standard army aviation scheme of olive drab and black. There are a variety of red and yellow warning markings, as well as the blue and red subdued national insignia. The Silver Eagles insignia is shown in the inset, above right. This marking is medium blue, with the eagle's head in silver and the trim in white.

47

Notes sur les planches en couleur

A1 Le fini plus coloré—gris olivâtre avec des marques jaunes et un panneau avant noir, le nez portant parfois des insignes de bataillon—allait devenir moins apparent durant la suite de la guerre. Le missile SS.11 est olivâtre, avec des marques jaunes indiquant un missile 'live', et l'appareil de lancement est gris clair. **A2** L'hélicoptère antichars aux meilleurs résultats, qui détruisit 18 chars, quatre canots et huit camions; les marques de destruction de chars sont rouges, les autres—difficiles à distinguer de l'arrière-plan—sont vertes. Noter également quelques petits badges blancs portant des têtes de mort à l'avant des lanceurs TOW.

B1 Le fini gris-sable très pâle de la plupart des véhicules et de tous les hélicoptères israéliens est rehaussé seulement par l'insigne national et par le 'V' jaune désignant l'opération 'Paix pour la Galilée' depuis 1982. **B2** Fini très similaire pour ce Cobra. La queue de l'appareil porte des marques d'escadrille ressemblant à une caricature, mais nous regrettons qu'elles soient classifiées et nous sommes forcés de les effacer sur la photo.

C1 Il s'agit apparemment d'une livraison standard par l'Aérospatiale de camouflage dans le désert: couleur jaune et verte avec une base gris-bleu. A noter le numéro de série et les insignes nationales syriennes. Les Israéliens rentrèrent en possession de cet hélicoptère après les combats de 1982. **C2** Les Cobras iraniens furent livrés dans un camouflage 'earth yellow' et 'field drab' avec une base grise. L'écusson qui figure sur le nez de l'appareil est celui du corps d'aviation de l'armée iranienne; depuis le renversement du schah, le sigle IIAA a été remplacé dans la plupart des cas—mais pas tous, semble-t-il—par le sigle IRIAA ('Islamic Republic of Iran Army Aviation'). Il y a lieu de remarquer la nouvelle visière M65 TOW.

D1 Cette machine iraquienne possède le même fini que la Gazelle syrienne, mais son camouflage est d'un vert plus foncé. L'application des insignes nationales iraquiennes diffère sensiblement d'une machine à l'autre. **D2** Variation standard de la livraison soviétique dans des tons de jaune/brun et de vert/brun; sur certains hélicoptères d'exportation, le signal d'avertissement figurant que la queue est en anglais, 'Danger'.

E1 Camouflage bariolé employé sur certains hélicoptères polonais, avec de simples marques nationales et un numéro tactique. **E2** Autre livraison standard Mil-24, de couleur jaune et vert foncé. Les numéros tactiques sont de différentes couleurs: on suppose l'existence d'un système de code d'escadrille, mais rien ne permet de le prouver. Les insignes rouges (détail, en haut à droite) figurent sur certains 'Hinds' et d'autres aéronefs tactiques; il pourrait s'agir d'un signe de capacité de vol pour unités de vol avant.

F1 Arrivées au Tchad dans le vert armée habituel, ces Gazelles ont été camouflées rapidement sous un fini improvisé couleur de boue assez clair. N'apparaît que la première des trois lettres blanches habituelles de la marque tactique de l'escadrille. (Détail, à droite) Insignes de la Force d'action rapide. **F2** La livraison 'Hind-A' grise et vert foncé, sur laquelle figurent seulement les insignes nationales lybiennes marquées par un disque vert. Sur certaines machines lybiennes, le camouflage des parties supérieures est répété sur les parties inférieures.

G1 Le vert est plus pâle que sur les la plupart des livraisons 'Hind'. A noter les insignes sandinistes habituelles et le nouvel éclair sur le plan de dérive. Cette machine est équipée du système dit 'hot-brick' destiné à la protéger contre les missiles SA-7 utilisés par les contre-rebelles. **G2** Un schéma uniforme très terne de vert forêt assorti de marques noires fut utilisé pour l'opération Grenada. Le dispositif qui figure sur les ailes auxiliaires est un 'countermeasures dispenser'.

H1 Modèle standard de couleur noire et neutre utilisé sur les PAH-1 et les BO-105, toutes les marques, à l'exception des signes d'avertissement, étant d'un noir adouci. **H2** Camouflage olivâtre et noir, comme sur la plupart des véhicules et des hélicoptères britanniques, avec des insignes nationales rouges et bleues adoucies et divers signes d'avertissement rouges et jaunes. Les insignes 'Silver Eagles' (détail, en haut à droite) sont de couleur bleu neutre, argent et blanc.

Farbtafeln

A1 Dieser farbenfreudigere Anstrich (olivgrau mit gelben Markierungen und eine schwarze Bugplatte, manchmal mit Bataillonsabzeichen) wurde im lauf des krieges weniger auffällig. Das SS.11 Gescho- ist olivfarben mit gelben Markierungen (als 'live'-Geschoss) und die Startanlage hellgrau. **A2** Der erfolgreichste Panzerabwehr-Hubschrauber aller Zeiten, der 18 Panzer, vier Boote und acht Lastwagen zerstörte; die Panzerabschussliste ist rot, die anderen Markierungen (vor dem Hintergrund schwer zu erkennen) grün. Man beachte die weiss Totenkopfabzeichen vorne auf den TOW Startern.

B1 Der blasse sandgraue Anstrich der meisten israelischen Fahrzeuge und aller Hubschrauber wird lediglich durch die Landesfarben aufgeheitert sowie durch das gelbe V für die Operation 'Frieden für Galiläa' (1982). **B2** Dieser Cobra trägt einen ähnlichen Anstrich. Kleine Cartoon-ähnliche Staffelabzeichen befinden sich auf dem Heck; die Ziffern unterliegen einer Informationssperre, daher ist die entsprechende Fläche auf diesem Bild freigelassen.

C1 Offenbar eine Standardausführung der Aérospatiale für Wüstentarnung: gelb und grün mit hellblauer Unterseite. Man beachte die Seriennummer und die syrischen Nationalzeichen. Dieser Hubschrauber wurde nach den Kämpfen von 1982 von den Israelis erbeutet. **C2** Iranische Cobras hatten eine Tarnung von 'earth yellow' und 'field drab' mit grauer Unterseite. Das Abzeichen auf dem Bug gehört zum Iranian Army Aviation Corps; nach der Absetzung des Schahs wurde die Abkürzung IIAA in den meisten, aber nicht in allen Fällen durch IRIAA ersetzt: Islamic Republic of Iran Army Aviation. Man beachte das neue M65 TOW Visier.

D1 Diese irakische Maschine, mit ähnlichem Anstrich wie die syrische Gazelle, hat ein dunkleres Grün als Tarnfarbe. Die Auftragung der irakischen Landesfarben ist bei den Maschinen jeweils verschieden. **D2** Standardvariation der sowjetischen Lieferung in blassgelb und grünen/braunen Tönen; bei einigen Exporthubschraubern ist die Warnung auf dem Heck in englisch angebracht, 'Danger'.

E1 Die farbenprächtige Tarnung bei einigen polnischen Hubschraubern mit einfachen Landesfarben und taktischer Nummer. **E2** Eine andere typische Mil-24 Lieferung mit gelb und dunkelgrün. Die taktischen Nummern haben unterschiedliche Farben; ein Staffel-Codesystem wird angenommen, ist aber noch nicht entschlüsselt. Die roten Abzeichen (Detail, oben rechts) finden sich auf einigen 'Hinds' und anderen taktischen Flugzeugen; es handelt sich möglicherweise um ein Leistungsabzeichen für Frontflugeinheiten.

F1 Diese Gazelles kamen im Tschad im normalen vert armée an und erhielten rasch eine improvisierte Tarnung in heller Schlammfarbe. Dadurch ist nur noch der erste der drei Buchstaben des taktischen Heckzeichens zu erkennen. (Detail, rechts): Abzeichen der Force d'Action Rapide. **F2** Die 'Hind-A' Lieferung in grau und dunkelgrün mit dem einfachen libyschen Nationalabzeichen auf einem grünen Kreis. Einige libysche Maschinen haben die Tarnfarben der Oberseiten auch auf der Unterseite.

G1 Das grün ist blasser als bei den meisten 'Hind' Lieferungen. Man beachte das normale Sandinista Nationalabzeichen und den neuen Blitz auf der Heckflosse. Diese Maschine hat das sogenannte 'hot brick'-System gegen die von den Contra-Rebellen benutzten SA-7 Geschosse. **G2** Ein eintöniges Schema von waldgrün mit schwarzen Markierungen wurde für die Grenada-Operation benutzt. Auf den Stummelflügeln sieht man den 'countermeasures dispenser'.

H1 Übliches mittleres und schwarzes Muster der PAH-1 und BO-105 mit allen Markierungen in gedämpftem Schwarz, abgesehen von den Warnzeichen. **H2** Olivgrau und schwarz sind die Tarnfarben wie bei den meisten britischen Fahrzeugen und Hubschraubern, mit gedämpften roten und blauen Landesabzeichen und verschiedenen roten und gelben Warnzeichen. Die 'Silver Eagles' Abzeichen (Detail, rechts oben) ist in mittlerem blau, silber und weiss gehalten.